Making
TikTok
Videos

WILEY

Making
TikTok
Videos

by Will Eagle with Hannah Budke,
Claire Cohen, Andrew Cooper,
Jordan Elijah Michael, and
Andrew Panturescu

WILEY

Making TikTok Videos For Dummies®

Published by: **John Wiley & Sons, Inc.**, 111 River Street, Hoboken, NJ 07030-5774, www.wiley.com

Contents

Project 3: Popular TikToks 29

Project 4: Making A TikTok 48

Glossary   170

INTRODUCTION

YOU'VE HEARD ABOUT TIKTOK, MAYBE YOU'VE ALREADY STARTED SPENDING HOURS SCROLLING THROUGH ALL THE AMAZING VIDEOS OUT THERE, AND NOW YOU'RE READY TO START MAKING YOUR OWN. This book tells you everything you need to know to get started making your own TikTok videos, along with expert tips on how to make the most out of your TikTok experience. There are millions and millions of people on TikTok, and they're all waiting to see what YOU make. Let's do this!

ABOUT TIKTOK

TikTok is really, really big. It's about a billion people every month using the app, which is enormous. There are so many videos or "TikToks," which we'll use interchangeably, out there with new videos created every minute.

A lot of people think that TikTok is just an app for lip synching and dancing kids, but that's only one part of TikTok. Sure, the platform started with people making dance videos, and that drew a big audience, contributing to TikTok's early popularity. But today, TikTok features millions of TikTokers making content about everything. Did you know that at the time of writing there were over 170 million creators on TikTok with an audience of 10,000 or more?

There are a few things that make TikTok very special:

» Anyone can have a hit video with hundreds of thousands of views or more!

» You can make content about almost anything, and you'll find an audience who loves you for it.

» It's really easy to get started creating and posting content.

» TikTok is even better with friends and family joining in on the fun.

We'll challenge you to think about what type of content you want to make. It's certainly best to choose something that you are truly passionate and knowledgeable about, and that it's something you think people will want to see.

TikTok is one of the most exciting video platforms out there, and an amazing chance to express your creativity, build an audience, and have a ton of fun. There are some smart precautions you will want to take, which we cover right out the gate in Project 1: Getting Started.

ABOUT THIS BOOK

This book has been written by TikTok experts, so you can feel confident you're getting good advice, but our top tip is to just get started and experiment. Follow along with the advice in this book but know that you'll learn so much just by starting to make your first of many TikToks. You can always save anything you make as a draft, without needing to make it live on TikTok for the world to see, which is a great way to practice.

In this book, you:

» Download the app and create your profile

» Learn how to search for and find inspiration

» Familiarize yourself with popular TikToks

» Record your TikTok and learn about advanced creation techniques

» Discover how to go LIVE and reach new fans

» Get tips on how to grow your audience

Some figures will have a magnifying glass, like you see here. The glass draws attention to the parts of the screen you'll use. The highlighted text draws your attention to the figure.

ABOUT YOU

You're looking to make TikTok videos, right? Great. You've come to the right place. If you already know your way around TikTok, you can skip some sections and just take what you need from this book. We've written this for those of you who are just getting started, all the way through to advanced users looking to grow their audience. Remember, though, your worth isn't all about likes and followers, so while growing an audience on TikTok is rewarding, it's not everything in life.

ABOUT ICONS

As you read through projects in this book, you'll see different icons appearing, which help identify important content. Look out for the following:

WARNING

Your safety is super important, so if something has the potential to be dangerous, we'll mark it with a warning icon. We'll give you advice on how to smartly navigate things.

REMEMBER

This icon is a handy reminder of the most important information to remember during a project. Think of this as the information you'll want to recall for the future.

TIP

There are tons of tips in this book, giving you inside advice on how to make the absolute best of the project you're working on.

IT MIGHT SEEM A BIT ANNOYING TO START YOUR TIKTOK ADVENTURE WITH A WHOLE CHUNK OF THIS BOOK DEDICATED TO SAFETY, SECURITY, AND LEGAL STUFF, BUT IT'S SUPER IMPORTANT TO KNOW SO YOU CAN MAKE SMART CHOICES.

The early days of TikTok were a bit of a wild west, meaning that sometimes the content wasn't what a parent would consider "safe" for their family, but TikTok is maturing a lot as a platform, and it's getting better and better at ensuring you have a fully safe and comfortable experience.

MAKING SMART CHOICES

When you're doing anything online, and especially when it comes to social media and video content creation, it's really important to know how to navigate safely. This might seem like boring stuff but knowing some of the safety basics will mean you are set up for success and can avoid unpleasant situations.

» If you're under 18, you will need permission from a parent or legal guardian to sign up and use TikTok.

» There is some important legal stuff to know to make sure you don't get into TikTok trouble.

» And most of all, you want to ensure everything you do on TikTok keeps you safe.

» A few minutes reading this section is time well spent.

GETTING PERMISSION

Ask your parent or legal guardian if you can download TikTok to your phone, tablet, or computer. It's a great idea to have a conversation with your parent about why you want to use TikTok, how you intend to use it, and how they can participate in your usage of TikTok to ensure you're enjoying your experience.

COPYRIGHT

You should have a basic understanding of copyright. If you write an original book, if you make an original movie, if you create an original TV show, and if you make an original TikTok video, you are the copyright owner of it. *Copyright* is a legal term that means you are the owner of something, and so someone else can't claim that they made it. Copyright only applies to original content you create — meaning, you made this and no one else, and copyright encourages people not to steal other people's original content creations. This means one simple thing: Don't use other people's work and pretend it's your own. For example, don't video record a TV show and post it on TikTok — they'll take it down immediately, and you might get some kind of strike against your account. Remember, only upload to TikTok content that you have created.

TIP

Okay, a copyright protects original content, but sounds are different — right? Well, TikTok has a big sound library that you can use to make your TikTok videos. Sounds are original content creations and remain the copyright of the legal owner, but TikTok and the copyright owners allow people to use their sounds in videos. We explore using sound in Project 4.

UNDERSTANDING SAFETY

Why all this emphasis on safety? Well, with any social media site, people are uploading content, and sometimes that content might have more adult themes unsuitable for someone younger. Further, the platform works hard to ensure nothing illegal is posted. People still try — every day — to upload content to apps like TikTok that they shouldn't. And because TikTok is a social media site, it's a place where you might find yourself talking with strangers, so proceed with caution.

TIP

Listen to your instincts. If you're unsure if something is appropriate, or if something is making you feel unsafe, ask your parent or legal guardian for their advice and help.

WARNING

Above all else, never give out your personal information like your phone number, e-mail address, or home address to anyone on the Internet without a parent or legal guardian's permission. And remember that you can block people if needed.

NAVIGATING THE APP

If you're completely new to TikTok, it's time to download the app and get familiar with the basics. We'll dive right in and cover:

» Downloading the app and creating your Profile

» Learning about privacy and security settings.

» Understanding viewing basics like Follows, Likes, Comments, and Shares

DOWNLOADING TIKTOK

Head to either the Apple App Store (iPhone) or the Google Play Store (Android) and search for TikTok and get started by downloading the app. After you've downloaded the TikTok app, open it to get started.

CREATING YOUR PROFILE

1 **When you open the app, you'll be asked to either log in (if you already have an account) or to sign up. Choose Sign up.**

2 **You'll choose from different options to sign up — using your phone number, e-mail address, or a Facebook or Google account.**

You might be asked to enter a code sent to either your phone or e-mail address for verification.

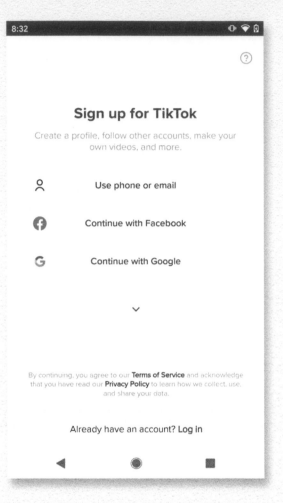

3 You'll be asked to enter your birthdate, as well as pass a verification security step (usually matching a puzzle piece to the right spot in an image).

4 **You'll create a username and password (if needed).**

You can change your username later if you'd like, but it's best to choose something and stick with it. You can use your name but consider using a fun nickname instead. If you have other social profiles, like Instagram, consider choosing the same username so people can find you across other social media platforms.

5 **You might be asked to choose your interests, such as Beauty & Fashion or Football.**

This will help TikTok show you content you are more likely to like.

6 **From any screen in the app, you can click on the Profile icon in the bottom-right corner. Here you can upload a profile photo, as well as edit your profile to add things like links to your other social profiles, your pronouns, a bio, and even a charity (or nonprofit) you support.**

Your profile displays how many people are following you, how many people you are following, and how many likes your videos have received to date.

TIP

We suggest using a photo of your pet or something inanimate like your favorite house plant, toy or any object. It's better for your privacy and lets you show your sense of humor.

PRIVACY

When you sign up for TikTok, you'll be asked to pass through what's known as an *age gate*. In the U.S. market, you need to be at least 13 years old to use most of TikTok's features. If you're **under 13 years old,** TikTok will place you in their TikTok for Younger Users experience, which has additional privacy and safety protections designed specifically for you. That's a good thing, so when you sign up, be honest about your age. We point out other legal requirements, like age requirements to live stream, in the later project chapters.

You'll have the option to customize your privacy settings in the app. Here's how to set up further privacy settings:

1 Tap the hamburger menu in the upper-right corner. (It looks like three horizontal stacked lines.)

2 Choose Settings and Privacy.

3 Choose Privacy.

In this section, you'll find options to:

» **Set your account to private.** With a private account, only users you approve can follow you and watch your videos. For maximum safety, consider setting your account to private.

» **Set your activity status.** When you turn this feature on, you and the followers you follow back will see each other's activity status.

» **Turn on/off suggesting your account to others.** TikTok will recommend your account to other people who might like to follow you. But you can turn this off at a few different levels including your contacts, your Facebook friends, people with mutual connections, and even people who open or send links to you.

» **Turn off location services.** TikTok is saying here that they use your geographic location to improve the content and ads they show you. Really this means they want to know your location for the best possible advertising targeting. You can turn this feature off, but TikTok will still guess your location using your Internet service provider and IP address (the address of your device on the Internet).

» **Customize your interactions.** You can play with settings around comments, mentions, tags, who can direct message you, duet and stitch you, accounts you may have blocked, and much more.

TAKING A QUICK LOOK AT THE FEATURES

When you open the TikTok app, you'll immediately see a video playing. You can scroll down to refresh your feed and tap the screen to pause it so we can look around at the different features.

» At the top of the app, you'll see two words — *Following* and *For You*. The Following page shows you content only from accounts you are following whereas the For You page shows you content recommended by the TikTok algorithm. (That's fancy speak for a computer program making choices on what to show you.) You can flip between either of these tabs to enjoy videos. We explain these tabs in more detail in "Project 2: Finding Inspiration."

» At any time, tap the Home button in the bottom-left corner to return to the home screen.

» There's a plus-sign button (+) used to create your own TikToks. Check out "Project 4: Making a TikTok" for more info.

On the right–hand side, you'll see a row of vertical icons. Let's start with the profile photo of the person who uploaded the video paused on your screen.

FOLLOW

Tap the "+" button under the profile photo and you'll immediately follow that person. Their content will appear on your Following page and will most likely show up on your For You page (or FYP). If you tap the upper part of their profile image, you'll be taken to their Profile page where you can see how many people are following them, who they follow, how many likes they have in total, and even links to message them on TikTok and on other social profiles.

LIKES

The heart icon shows how many times people have liked the video. You can only like a video once. Tap the heart once to "Like," and again to remove the Like. There isn't a "Dislike" button. But if you tap and hold anywhere on the screen, there is a "Not interested" option that enables you to teach TikTok what content you don't like. Make use of the Like and Not interested features to make TikTok show you more of the content you love.

COMMENTS

The next icon looks like a chat bubble and has the number of comments that the video has received. You can tap this icon to see what people have said, add your own comment, and like or reply to other people's comments.

FAVORITES

The button that looks like a ribbon is your bookmark button to save your favorites. You'll find your saved favorites listed on your profile. Just tap the profile icon in the bottom-right corner. Just beneath your bio, you'll see a row of four icons. The heart icon shows you videos you have liked, and the bookmark icon shows you videos you have marked as your favorites.

SHARES

The arrow icon lets you share the video with your friends. Tap this and choose to repost the video, copy the link, or send it to one of your messaging or social media apps. You can even save the video, actually downloading a copy of the video itself, and take other actions like duet or stitch, which we cover in "Project 2: Finding Inspiration."

SOUNDS

The last icon on the right side looks like a spinning wheel. Tap that icon and you'll see what sound is used in the TikTok. You can add this sound to your favorite sounds, or you can immediately record it by tapping "Use this sound." Skip ahead to "Project 4: Making a TikTok" for more on how to use sounds to make your own TikTok.

TIP

The app changes over time with new features and buttons, but the principles remain the same. If you find something has changed in the app that doesn't line up with the instructions in this book, it's likely that the button has simply moved to a new location.

EQUIPMENT YOU'LL NEED

You already have it in your hand. (No, not this book, although that's definitely a handy piece of equipment.) All you need is a phone or tablet to be able to use and make TikToks. If you have other equipment, like a ring light that provides great lighting, then that's great, but it's not necessary to make great content.

PROJECT 2 FINDING INSPIRATION

READY TO FIND SOME INSPIRATION? You've come to the right section. The authors of this book spend hundreds of hours on TikTok each week, so you don't have to.

The best part of TikTok is that inspiration is everywhere (and we mean **everywhere**). Whether you're browsing your FYP (For You page), searching for the trend you saw last week, or looking for something new, you're bound to find inspiration at every scroll. Here are ways to make the most out of your search and find inspiration every time you open the app.

USING THE SEARCH BAR

The search bar is your secret sauce. Think of the search bar as the public library of TikTok. It houses all the knowledge and videos you could ever be looking for. You can:

» Search for videos you've seen in the past 7 days, so if you can't find that TikTok you saw last night that is stuck in your head, have no fear. In the below figure, you'll see that you can use the "Filter" button in the top-right corner to pull up a series of filters to help you find the video you're looking for. You can toggle on "Watched videos" to only filter through videos you've seen in the past week, so you never have to worry about losing a video you thought was great! You can toggle on videos made this week, if you're trying to hop on a trend, or search by "most liked" to find big, trending videos you may have missed.

» Search using full sentences or fragments

» Search words from trending songs

» See trending hashtags or video themes

» Find inspiration for anything — what to make for a snack, what show to binge watch tonight, how to do your math homework (yes, seriously), and so much more

» Search for pop culture drama and tea about your favorite celebs

Next time you open TikTok, check out the search feature to discover a whole world of content you didn't even know existed.

TIP

Check out the sidebar "Narrowing Down Your Ideas" in Project 4 for further tips on finding inspiration and developing your creative ideas.

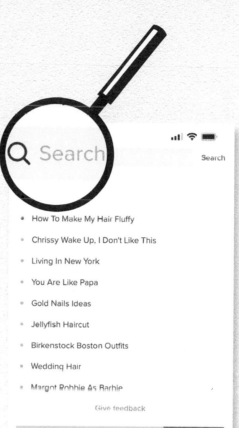

- How To Make My Hair Fluffy
- Chrissy Wake Up, I Don't Like This
- Living In New York
- You Are Like Papa
- Gold Nails Ideas
- Jellyfish Haircut
- Birkenstock Boston Outfits
- Wedding Hair
- Margot Robbie As Barbie

Give feedback

TIP

Searching on TikTok will help TikTok's algorithm get to know you better. This isn't anything to be afraid of; it just means you're more likely to get content you enjoy at every scroll. As you search, TikTok learns about what you like and dislike, and helps create a better user experience for you! This is why everyone's FYP is so different, because everyone has their own interests, humor, and style.

TIP

Running out of inspiration? The search bar has some trending audios, hashtags, and challenges automatically populated at the bottom, so you're sure to never miss out on a trend.

TOP VIDEOS

Top videos will change by the day, but you can rest assured that by scrolling on your FYP, you will encounter the top videos. Looking for a place to start? Use the top TikTok user's content to see what they're up to. Seeing the same audio come up? Maybe you've seen the same dance a few times? It's probably trending! Tap on the spinning wheel (the sound) and see how many videos have been made with it. If there's only a few thousand, congrats! You might be early to a trend. Keep an eye on that audio to watch it explode, or better yet, get in on the action. Make a TikTok with this audio to ride the wave of a trend you caught early. If there are already tens of thousands of videos under that sound, you've found an already trending audio. The good news is it's never too late to hop on a trend! Make a video quickly and get it posted for your best chances of going viral.

TOP USERS

The best thing about TikTok is how it learns about you. So, you may see the same people come up on your FYP often. This doesn't mean they're Top Users nationally or globally, but rather creators that you've liked, engaged with, and maybe even followed. Worldwide, current TikTok royalty includes: The D'Amelio family (led by Charli), Bella Poarch (creator who took her unique head bopping videos and turned herself into an absolute star), and Addison Rae (dancer turned celeb all-star). There's also no shortage of family creators, like The

McFarlands, a family all about fun, and the LaBrants, who rose to fame with dad Cole LaBrant and eventually became a family household name.

REMEMBER

By the time you read this, there may be a new head TikToker in town, and that's the best part of the platform — there's room for everyone at the top of the FYP. One of the many things people love about TikTok is that there's truly room for everyone to be successful and have fun!

The best part about top users is that they're often posting the trends (and starting them). Following them is a way to ensure you're not missing out on the top TikTok trends of the week.

POPULAR VIDEOS

Popular videos change overnight. Trends are in a revolving door of coming and going. On TikTok, what is popular on Monday may be out of trend by Friday. The best way to find trending videos is to simply scroll your FYP. You may notice that a video you have scrolled upon has millions of likes, which tells you it's a popular video. Plus, then there's a greater chance your friends will have seen that video, too.

Currently, there are themes of popular content, divided into different categories. For example, in the category of style and fashion, GRWM (Get Ready with Me) currently rules the space. This is typically videos of creators trying on their latest shopping haul or getting ready for an event. They'll often talk to the camera, like they're talking directly to their audience (to "give it a try" or "it's a great style for . . ."). In the category of technology, direct to camera reviews reign supreme. This usually looks like your favorite influencer talking directly to the camera and sharing their opinions of the newest gadgets. And in the lifestyle category, everyone loves a good vlog (video blog about their day), where creators take their followers with them through their daily routines.

TIP

Spend some time scrolling your FYP to find trending themes in videos.

If something is happening in real life (like the Olympics, for example) you can be sure that Olympics content will be not only the most popular, but TikTok will push that content out. TikTok always wants to be culturally relevant, so any top world events will be top of the FYP. Making content surrounding that event might have a greater chance of increasing views.

TIP

TRENDING SOUNDS

Audio is a huge part of TikTok. They say trends start on TikTok, and they are not kidding. Chances are the buzzy song that you can't get out of your head is a TikTok trend. Go to the TikTok search bar and type in "trending sounds" and then be amazed at all the great content you can find. TikTok will list the top trending songs for you, right at your fingertips.

You can use any **trending sound** and apply it to whatever content you want to make. Do you love to cook? Take a trending audio and put it in the background of your next cooking video. Learning hip hop in dance class? Make a dance to the latest trending audio and watch your views go up. Making a daily vlog? Use your favorite artist's newest song.

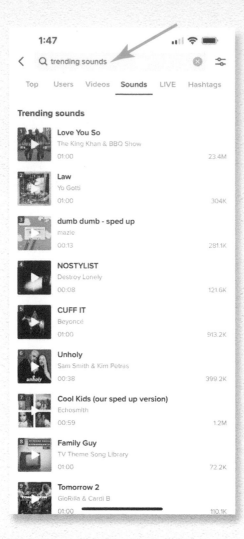

Have you ever seen a video where the audio is a story time? This is because you're more likely to watch and listen when interesting things are happening to both your eyes and ears. Pair your next cooking video with a viral clip of someone spilling the tea on a topic to boost views.

If you're talking in the video, be sure the song's audio is set to a lower volume than your talking audio; otherwise it will be hard for people to hear you (and you always want people to be able to hear you!)

LIVE STREAMERS

Live streaming is a great way for creators to connect with their audience on a much more casual and personal level. It's a chance for you to be authentic with your followers and let them peek behind the curtain to see what you're all about. See Project 5 for full details on how to go LIVE.

» Go LIVE multiple times a week to allow your followers to get used to you being live.

» Open up a Q&A (questions and answers) when on live stream to encourage people to comment and ask questions. (This will boost engagement with your audience and tell TikTok that people are loving your live stream, and then TikTok will push it to more users.)

» Think about adding a visual element to every live video. More people are inclined to watch if you do an AMA (ask me anything) while getting ready, baking a cake, etc. Keeping watchers entertained is the most important thing about going live. You want to be attracting new watchers every second to build your live viewership over time.

TIP

Remember, you have to be at least 16 years old (or have a parent or guardian present) and have 1,000 followers or more to go LIVE.

HASHTAGS

Hashtags are a powerful tool if you can utilize them correctly. Currently, brands can pay a pretty penny to have a "hashtag challenge (HTC)." You know a brand is participating in an HTC when you see a custom emoji next to it, see it in the search bar, or see it auto populate when you go to upload a new video.

Hashtags are a great way to find more people who are interested in your content. For example, if you make a cooking video, hashtag things like #cooking and #homemadedinner, to get more eyes on your content.

The beauty of hashtags on TikTok is that you don't need them to grow a video, but they help you bring in viewers who are looking for that type of content. So, using a well-known hashtag like #fyp might bring in viewers who might not see your videos otherwise. There's more information about the FYP in the next section.

TIP

Remember how we mentioned hashtag challenges? Well, those hashtags are great to use because when a brand pays TikTok to have a custom hashtag, they want all the eyeballs they can possibly get on it. This will only help your content, and make sure you're getting the max reach, but be careful, these hashtags will change every few days, so be sure to keep your eyes peeled for the latest and greatest.

TIP

Having trouble finding them? Look to your FYP and scroll until you find unique, branded hashtags that sound something like #PepsiChallenge. Usually, it will include the brand first, and the "challenge" second.

Check out Project 4 for details on how to add more hashtags when you're posting your first video; you'll find more hashtags are recommended to you when you're publishing a video.

TIP

THE FOR YOU PAGE (FYP)

The FYP, better known as the For You page, is well . . . created just for you! When scrolling the FYP, you'll never reach the end. You'll be able to find a slew of content that is entertaining, funny, and pulls at the heartstrings — all at once. To find inspiration here, our best suggestion is to simply scroll. The algorithm will learn more about you the more you scroll, paying attention to the things you like, comment on, send to friends, and rewatch. No need to be worried, this is just the internal algorithm making sure you have a good time on TikTok. It will learn more about you as time goes on, so don't get discouraged if your FYP isn't knocking it out of the park on day one. It will take some time for it to get to know you, so be patient and keep engaging with the content you love.

Find content you don't want to see? You can press or hold down on the video and a box will pop up where you can click "Not interested." This will help the algorithm not serve you content that you don't like. Treat your FYP like a new friend; it's just trying to get to know you.

TIP

THE FOLLOWING PAGE

The following page is what TikTok is most known for historically. It is a constant scroll of people you have selected to follow. The following page pushes you content only from people you're following — meaning your friends, family, and favorite influencers. This is where you can see the videos your friends made at lunch, the new song your sister is dropping, and all the content that people you've chosen to follow have made. The best part of the following page? No ads! (So far . . .) This is a great tab to use when you want to stay in the loop with friends, but we always suggest branching out and scrolling your FYP, because you'll see your friends' content there as well, but you will also see a world of other content from users you don't follow.

THE FRIENDS PAGE

A new addition to the TikTok user experience is the Friends page. The icon is at the bottom of the screen. This is content only from people you follow *and* who follow you back. This is a great place to go if you want to keep up with your friends. If you make a TikTok that is only visible to friends, this is where it will show up for them.

PROJECT 3 POPULAR TIKTOKS

KNOWING WHERE TO START CAN BE OVERWHELMING, BECAUSE THERE IS NO LIMIT TO THE TIKTOKS YOU COULD POTENTIALLY MAKE. A great starting point is to look at TikToks that have been historically very popular, as those are pretty much tried-and-true classics that people still love to watch in the app.

REMEMBER

Consider practicing making TikToks by first copying some classic TikTok trends, as there are lots of examples out there.

CLASSIC DANCES

Did you know TikTok started out as an app called Musica.ly? Musica.ly was the super fun app that eventually became TikTok; it mostly featured people lip syncing and dancing, which made dancing truly the roots of TikTok. Making a dance video is one of the best places to start when making your TikToks. Here are some of the absolute best classic dances. Search within the TikTok app to find them:

» **Say So:** Originally created by Haley Sharpe (@yodelinghaley) back in December of 2019, this TikTok dance features the Doja Cat classic. At the time of writing, Hayley had 3.5 million followers on TikTok with over 225 million likes of her content.

» **Savage:** Arguably one of the hits that made Megan Thee Stallion's career take off into superstardom, the Savage dance was created by @keke.janajah. You'll recognize the lyrics because they are savage, classy, boujie, ratchet . . .!

» **Blinding Lights:** This dance creation is credited to @macdaddyz to *Blinding Lights* by Canadian superstar

The Weeknd. It's sure to put a smile on your face while you're dabbing and bouncing on your toes. Search for Blinding Lights and The McFarlands for a truly excellent example, which had 2.4 million likes at the time of writing.

» **Renegade:** The song for this classic dance is *Lottery* by K Camp, and features complex choreography, but we believe in you, you can do this. Search on TikTok for Renegade Dance and look out for Charli D'Amelio's videos, as she's a big reason this dance took off, although credit should be given to the original creator of the dance, Jalaiah Harmon.

» **Create your own:** You don't need to feel limited to existing classic dances, or even recreating the latest trending dance. You can create your own! Who knows, maybe your dance will take off, and you'll become the latest viral sensation on the Internet.

TIP

Find more dances by going to the search feature in the TikTok app, search "dance trends" and include the year, for example, "dance trends 2023" and try something new!

LEARN THE FLOSS

The Floss is one of the top classic dances of all time on TikTok, and it's considered very much a "basic" dance that everyone should know how to do. Maybe you already know how to do this dance; you'll be the star of your friend's group if you can bust out the moves whenever a song comes on and you Floss. Hey, you could even be the one to teach your friends and make a group dance video. If you're not a natural dancer, don't worry, anyone can learn. Search in TikTok for "Floss Dance" and look for a slowed down tutorial video. Here's a step-by-step guide with visuals to help you break down all the movements. It might feel tough at first, but don't give up. You can do it!

1 **With your feet shoulder-width apart put your hands in fists kept at your sides. Turn to face the front of the room with your shoulders square.**

It's called the floss because with your hands in fists it looks like you're holding a big piece of string, like a large piece of dental floss. Slightly bend your knees to stay flexible and loose.

(continued)

(continued)

2 In a smooth fast motion, sweep your arms to the right across your body, keeping your arms nice and straight and your hands in fists.

3 At the same time, move your hips to the right as you are swinging your arms down in the opposite direction (to the left). You're moving your hips through your arms side to side (not back and forth.)

You can push your hips out as far as you like, but the closer you keep them to the center, the faster you can move. Push them further out for more drama!

4 Now, move your arms back up to the right, swinging your hips through them again. It's what you just did before but in the opposite direction. You'll find your hips are back where they were, and your arms will be to the right.

(continued)

(continued)

5 **In a sweeping motion, move both arms down in front of your body to your left. Keep your arms straight, and your hands should remain in fists.**

You're now in position to repeat the swinging movement of the Floss but on the other side. Keep your arms and fists close to your body so they almost brush your hips.

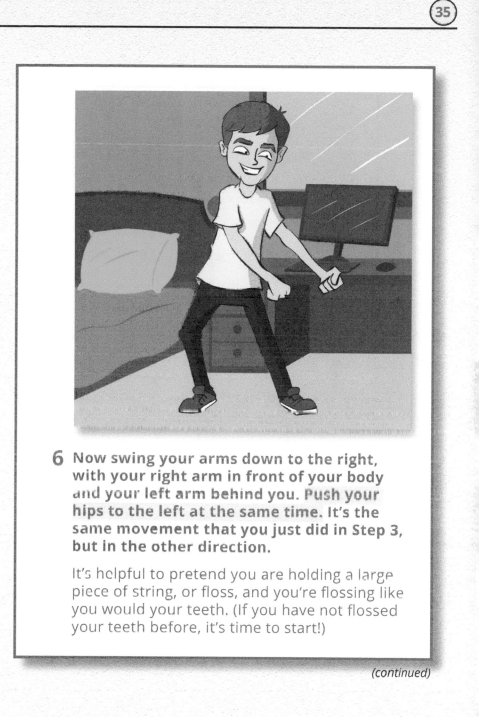

6 **Now swing your arms down to the right, with your right arm in front of your body and your left arm behind you. Push your hips to the left at the same time. It's the same movement that you just did in Step 3, but in the other direction.**

It's helpful to pretend you are holding a large piece of string, or floss, and you're flossing like you would your teeth. (If you have not flossed your teeth before, it's time to start!)

(continued)

(continued)

7 Move your arms back up to the left, swinging your hips through them again. It's what you just did in Step 4 but in the opposite direction. You'll find your hips are back where they were, and your arms will be to the left.

8 Sweep your arms to the other side and repeat the motion of swinging your hips and arms and speed things up as much as you can.

The faster you go, the better your Floss.

(continued)

(continued)

CHALLENGES

Challenge TikToks are just that — a great way to challenge yourself to something new while making great content at the same time.

Here are some to try out:

» **Stand Up Using One Leg:** If you're looking for a physical challenge, sit on the floor and try to stand up but only using one leg. It sounds easy but is incredibly hard. If you can do it, well done! Your core strength must be strong.

» **Tell Me Without Telling Me:** An easier type of challenge TikTok, this is a very popular trend. Start by searching for "Tell me without telling me" and watch some of the videos before picking one that appeals to you. It could be "Tell me you're lazy, without telling me you're lazy" and then you show people your messy bedroom.

» **Sing with Me:** One of the most fun challenges out there regardless of your singing ability, the Sing with Me challenge features a TikToker setting you up to be their duet partner. They'll pick a song, give you a starting note so you know which note to sing, and the lyrics will display on screen. You'll sing some parts, they'll sing other parts, and together you might sing at the same time. It's an easy way to learn how to deliver a beautiful duet with someone!

» **This Year I Will:** The "In 2022 I Will" TikTok challenge spread like wildfire with millions of posts just before the New Year celebrations. Each year you can state your new year's resolutions for this challenge.

WARNING

Be careful with challenges. In 2021, a dangerous challenge called the "Milk Crate Challenge" emerged where people climbed on top of stacked milk crates, which are wobbly and prone to collapsing. If you search for this challenge now, TikTok will display a warning message about safety along with safety resources, without even letting you see the challenge. They know that some challenges are dangerous and they don't want you to be harmed.

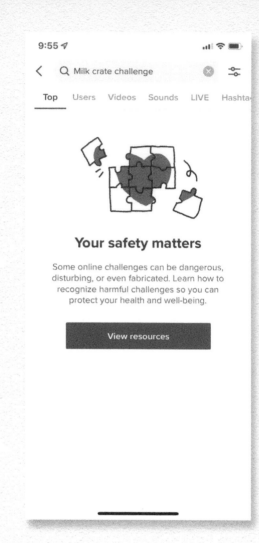

PRANKS

Everyone loves to go to TikTok to escape the real world, and that means we want to laugh. Pranks are a great way to bring the laughs in a way that keeps your content light.

THE WATER BOTTLE PRANK

Search *Water Bottle Prank* and you'll find tons of inspiration for different kinds of pranks involving water. For this prank, place a bottle of water over the penny, making sure the cap of the bottle is off. Then cover the bottle of water with a cloth and tell your friend that by saying some magic words the penny will magically go into the bottle. Say the magic words ("Hocus pocus," for example), pull off the cloth, and put your eye close up to the mouth of the bottle so you can look in. Exclaim to your friend that the penny is now in the bottle. When they go to look, squeeze the bottle so the water hits them in the face. This can be messy so consider doing it outside.

THE WATER AND BROOM PRANK

While your friend is in another room so they don't see, fill a bowl with water, stand on a chair, and hold the bowl of water on the ceiling using the broom handle to keep it in place. (Best to get permission for this one first.) Remove the chair, making sure it's not accessible to your friend, but keep holding the broom handle so the bowl of water stays in place. Call your friend to "Come hold this for a minute" and then leave them holding the broom with the bowl of water pressed against the ceiling. If they question you, you could say something like "I caught a spider in here, let me just go find something to cover the bowl so I can take it outside." Then just walk away. It's now on them to figure out how to stop holding the broom without the water crashing down on them.

THE TOILET'S RUNNING PRANK

A safer prank to play with water bottles because no one gets wet. Instead, say to your parent, with some urgency, that there's water coming out of the toilet.

They'll assume there's a leak. Instead, you've placed water bottles in a line, like a procession, from the toilet heading out of the bathroom. The joke is that "water is coming out of the toilet" without there being a leak. Dad's love and hate this joke in equal measure.

REMEMBER

If you're going to prank someone, make sure you do it safely. You don't want to surprise someone and have them accidentally hurt themselves, or damage things by getting water everywhere. Pranks are the most fun when they are harmless and silly, not serious or dangerous. A handy trick to know if your prank is a good one is to ask yourself "What would my reaction be if I were the one being pranked this way?"

LIP SYNCS

Why do we love lip syncs? Because a lip sync is the simplest way to hop on a trending audio. Have you ever been scrolling, and you see a lip sync sound multiple times? Chances are, it's a trending audio. Click on the spinning wheel in the bottom-right corner to see all the videos made with that sound.

Ready to hop on the trend? From the audio page, click "use this audio," and you'll be taken to make a TikTok, with that sound already added into the background. Easy peasy!

Lip syncs can be used as silly ways to hop on trends — maybe the Kardashians had a viral sound bite that is now making the rounds through comedy TikTok. Or maybe there is an important message from a politician you want to share with their audio. Maybe a DJ has mixed your favorite song and a popular line from your favorite show together, or maybe it's a lip sync challenge, where you show your stuff by lip syncing the lyrics or parts of a song. Lip syncs are among the most popular of content, so practice first and get to posting!

Practice makes perfect, and we mean it. Practice the audio tens, if not hundreds of times, to make sure you get it correct. Be sure to capture the breaths, pauses, and accents correctly. Accuracy is important when it comes to lip syncs, because they can often become viral when done well.

DUETS AND STITCHES

Duets and stitches may be the most powerful part of TikTok — and they are unique to the platform too!

Duets allow you to make a video that's side by side to an original video, which is great for adding in your facial expressions, reactions, commentary, and more. Think of it like a split screen, with you on one side, and the original video on the other. For example, a musical artist might make a TikTok called an "open verse challenge," where they sing part of their song and then leave a spot for you to write in your own lyrics. This is great for showing your skills and making your talent known to the world. If you have something to share, you should duet them!

Another popular form of content is "Stitch this and . . ." where a creator will make a video talking directly to the camera and say something like "Stitch this with your hidden talent." Then you can stitch (add) your video and show off your unique talent. This type of content happens all the time and is the perfect way to get extra views on your videos because you're already attaching yourself to a popular TikTok. Stitches increase your chances of being found.

Let's say you see a video of someone making a dance to a Doja Cat song; you can stitch it to show your choreography. If you see someone making something yummy for dinner, you can stitch it with your best try at the recipe.

Duets and stitches are a unique way to bring people together. They allow you to put your content together right next to someone else's. This is often used for feel-good content, talent challenges, or sentimental moments that will have you shedding a tear. But you don't have to stop there. Some stitch content is humorous and makes you laugh, poking fun at the original video, or even parodying it.

TIP

Be careful here; always make sure content is kind. Don't make fun of things people can't change, or anything that could make the original video creator feel unnecessarily bad about themselves.

MORE TIKTOKS TO MAKE

There are a lot more TikToks you can make. Try out some of these:

GRWM

GWRM means "get ready with me" and is an incredibly popular type of video on TikTok. In a classic GRWM, you'll introduce yourself, tell us what you're getting ready for, and start stepping us through the process. For example, let's say you're getting ready for school. You might show us how you choose what to wear, model some outfits for us, and then show us you in the final selection. You might brush or comb your hair and apply some lip balm. Then, show us how you pack your school bag. Once you're ready, let us know you're finished and ask your audience what they'd like to see for your next GRWM video.

STORY TIME

Making a story time TikTok is a fun and easy way to tell people about an interesting story that happened to you. In this TikTok, you're usually sitting down and facing the camera. You could be sitting anywhere, although you'll see a lot of folks telling their stories when they are sitting in a car. The trend just evolved that way, with people telling a story that just happened to them, for example, in a store or whilst out running an errand. It's simple: Think of your most interesting story and tell us what happened! It's best if there's a reveal or twist in the story, something truly interesting and surprising that makes this one of your best stories to tell.

UNBOXING

If you've saved your allowance and bought yourself a shiny new toy, especially something in tech or beauty, an unboxing video will have you taking us through the entire experience — from opening the box it came in to showing us around the item. For example, maybe you're a budding photographer and you just received a new lens as a gift. Show us the box, tell us what's inside, show us you are opening the box from different angles, then take your audience through the product itself, providing us with your review of how you use it, its features and whether you like it or not.

LISTS

Lists always make for popular content on any video platform. It's as simple as picking a topic, for example, "The Most Haunted Houses in America," then researching the topic and developing your script where you count down from, say, 10 to 1.

If you have a long list, consider breaking your video into parts.

TIP

RECIPES

Are you a good cook? Even the simplest of recipes make for great TikToks. Show us the step-by-step process you take to cook your favorite dish.

This is a great type of video to make with a parent or guardian. You can both star in your recipe TikToks.

TIP

ROUTINE AND DAY IN MY LIFE

Do you have a particularly interesting routine you, *errr*, routinely follow? Take us through your routine step by step. For example, you might always follow the same routine when you're warming up for soccer practice, getting ready for school, settling in for homework, or even tidying your room. A variant of this type of TikTok is "Day in my life" videos, where you take us through your entire day, whether it's a routine day or different from what you normally do.

TUTORIAL

A tutorial video is just what it sounds like, a chance for you to teach someone something you know.

1 **Pick your topic.** Pick something you're passionate and knowledgeable about, and that you think people are interested in learning about.

2 **Do some research.** Research the topic on YouTube, Google, and TikTok. You might find content that will help you in planning your own video.

3 Map out the steps. Write down all the key points, steps, and information you need to communicate in the video in the order it should be communicated. You can either use bullet points to remind yourself of the content you need to cover, or you can write a script for your entire video.

4 Gather the tools needed. Visuals, props, or any other types of tools can help with your tutorial. This helps bring more interest to your video and keep people's attention.

5 Film in a single take or in segments. You can film your tutorial live in one shot, or you can follow the steps you mapped out in Step 3 to film as segments, which can make it easier to film and edit.

TIP

At the end of your tutorial video, let people know to follow you so they can find more of your tutorial videos.

HAUL

Do you love to go on shopping sprees for new school clothes? Or did your feet grow and so it's time for *box-fresh* new sneakers? Then bring home your shopping bags and show us what's inside with your haul video. Search TikTok for "haul" if you've not seen a haul video before. The idea is simple:

1 You go shopping. A haul video typically features *a lot* of things, not just one purchase. Because sometimes you need to *treat yo' self.*

2 Show us what you bought and where you bought it from. Take us through the bags and boxes, being sure to show us the details including how things are packaged. Tell us about the experience you had in store. Try on your new clothes or accessories. What do you like about them?

PROJECT 4 MAKING A TIKTOK

NOW IT'S TIME FOR THE FUN PART! In this project, you learn how to make a plan for your first or next TikTok, a step-by-step process for recording, how to add sounds and edit like the pros, and how to post it so you can increase its views on TikTok. Whether you're new to posting or someone who posts regularly, this section covers it all.

TIP

The app changes over time with new features and buttons, but the principles remain the same. If you find something has changed in the app that doesn't line up with the instructions in this book, it's likely that the button has simply moved to a new location.

RECORDING YOUR FIRST TIKTOK

It's time to make your first TikTok! You might feel a bit nervous, excited, or maybe a mix of the two. But don't worry, read on for everything you need to know to make the TikToks you'd want to see on your For You page.

MAKING A PLAN

Before posting a TikTok, you'll want to take some time to think about the content of your video. Think back to Projects 2 and 3 in this book. Is there a type of popular TikTok that you'd want to try making yourself? Is there a trend you'd want to take part in? An audio you know you'd want to use?

If you can't think of anything right away, start thinking about the things you like to do. If you like to play soccer, try out a video showcasing your favorite drills. If you have a lot of hot takes on the latest Netflix show, make a TikTok to share them. Even if you like something as specific as drinking Shirley Temples, there's a place on TikTok for you.

You could also consider the content you like to watch on TikTok. If it's cooking videos, maybe you could try making them too. Or if you live on #fashionTikTok, start thinking about the biggest trends in the community and the types of videos you can make.

You don't need to be an expert in a certain category to start posting about it. In fact, it's often fun to see creators' journeys as they start learning more and more about a subject *by posting about it.*

TIP

Once you have your subject, start thinking about when and where you want to record. The beauty of TikTok is that it's a no-frills app — you don't need a fancy background or the newest phone to post. Your filming plan may depend on what type of content you're recording. For example, if you're sharing a *Storytime* video, you'd likely record that in a quiet place by yourself. However, if you were posting a "day in my life" video, you might use your phone camera to record a bunch of short videos from every part of your day.

RECORDING OPTIONS

There are usually two options for recording — you can record within the TikTok app or use your phone to record videos and upload them to the app later. Generally, it's recommended to record TikTok videos within the app when you want to film a small number of clips one right after each other (think: a storytime video or a product review). On the other hand, it's recommended to record your TikTok using your phone's camera when you're using a bunch of video clips, and a lot of time may pass between filming each clip (think: a montage of your favorite videos of your dog or a travel diary).

The process of recording your TikTok can be as complicated as you'd like, and will often depend on how much content you want to film and the quality you're looking for. Instructions are below for how to record a simple, no-frills TikTok but don't worry, we'll get into all the bells and whistles of music and editing later in the chapter.

To record and upload your TikTok:

1 **Open the TikTok app.**

2 **On the bottom of your home screen, hit the "+" button, which will take you to a page where you can record your own TikTok.**

3 **Record your video content by holding down the Record button — the red circle at the bottom of the screen.**

4 **If you'd like to upload content you've filmed on your phone, hit the Upload button next to the Record button.**

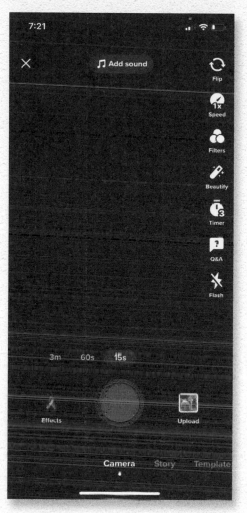

TIP

At any point you can save your video as a draft, so you don't have to post right away. This is a great way to capture your content and save it for editing later.

USING SOUNDS

Most people watch TikTok with the sound on, so choosing the right audio for your TikTok is key. Often videos using trending audios will get boosted more than others, so using a popular sound can offer a leg up in going viral.

To add a sound to your video, hit the button on the top of the Record page that says "Add Sound." The Discover page is also a great place to start, as it usually contains some of the most popular sounds on TikTok at that moment.

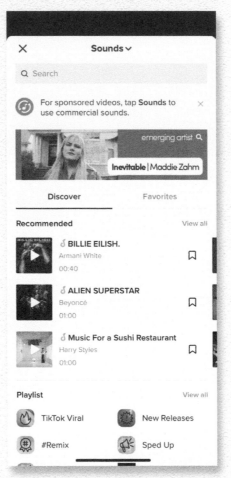

You can also check out the Playlists section right below it to browse songs grouped by category. The TikTok

Viral playlist is a great destination to browse some of the most popular songs on the app.

Once you've found some song options, think a bit about the vibe you want your audio to bring to your TikTok. Play something that speaks directly to what you're doing in the video by matching the sound to your content. For example, you might choose Chicken Teriyaki by Rosalía for your cooking video. Maybe you want something that's just great background music without too much loud audio (for example, Monkeys Spinning Monkeys is a popular favorite.)

TIP

Always keep an eye out for audio that you like while scrolling through TikTok. You can save any audio for your own future use; just click on the music icon in the bottom-left corner of the home screen. (You'll see the audio name next to it as well.) From there you can hit the "use this sound" button if you're ready to record with it right away, or hit "Add to Favorites" to find it in your favorited audio folder later.

APPLYING EFFECTS

Effects are just what they sound like; different types of visual effects that you can apply to your TikToks. Effects help you follow trends, enhance your videos, and are just plain fun to play around with. This section will discuss where to find different TikTok effects, how they work, and how to apply them to your videos.

THE EFFECTS LIBRARY

One of the easiest ways to create a TikTok is to record yourself trying out a popular effect on the app. Often effects are paired with a trend on the app, so it's always a good idea to see how other people are using the effect to help you prepare for your video.

To access the effects library:

1 Open the TikTok app.

2 Hit the "+" button at the bottom of the screen.

3 In the bottom-left corner, hit the "Effects" button.

4 Start playing around with all the magical effects!

TRENDING EFFECTS

The "Trending" effects is the first tab of options you'll see on the "Filters" page. Click on each one and try out the different effects. You might be able to draw something with your nose, create a mini-me, or show a backdrop with a bunch of sparkles or polka dots. Play around with them to see if adding an effect could amp up your TikTok or see if you want to hop on how other people are using a **trending effect**.

NEW EFFECTS

Next to the Trending tab you'll see the "New" effects tab which, you guessed it, shows the most recently added effects in the library. Often these will be related to events happening at the current time period (think: an effect that puts hearts in your eyes around Valentine's Day or an effect that gives you a Santa beard around the holidays). There may not be trends paired to certain effects yet so you'll have an opportunity to start a new trend!

POPULAR EFFECTS

While many effects come and go, there are some always-popular effects that you may want to incorporate in your videos:

» **Green screen:** This effect lets you record yourself talking in front of a background of your choice. You can choose one of TikTok's suggested backgrounds or select a photo from your camera roll to use as the background. There's an entire tab dedicated to different green screen options so try on a few to see what works best for your video.

» **What ___ are you:** These filters — which will tell you everything from "what bagel are you" to "where will you be in five years" — are especially fun (and easy!) to add to a video. Simply hit the effect, press the record button, and capture your reaction as the effect tells you your destiny.

» **Quizzes and games:** These are interactive effects that might ask you trivia questions, or have you choose your favorite among two things. Typically, you'll "wear" these effects on your forehead and tilt your head to one side to choose between different items.

WARNING

You'll notice that a lot of effects can change your appearance. While it can be fun to see what you'd look like with pink hair or rainbow eyelashes or different eye colors, remember that you don't need to use filters to post on TikTok. You're a beautiful person inside and out, and one of the wonderful things about TikTok is the community's acceptance of everyone's authentic, unfiltered selves.

SPECIAL TOOLS

On the **right side of the Record page**, you'll see a vertical list of tools you can use to help make your TikTok unique:

» **Flip** allows you to flip your camera view from the front to the back camera as needed.

» **Speed** lets you record content in slow motion (.3x and .5x) or in ultra-fast speed (2x and 3x). Most TikToks are filmed in the standard "1x" speed.

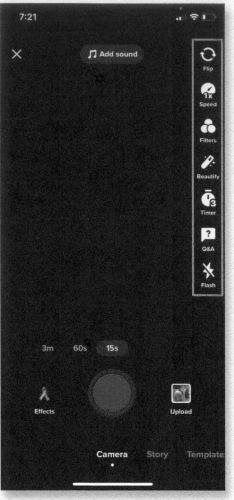

» **Filters** allow you to add a filter to the content you record to change its appearance. They have different categories that specialize in enhancing food, landscapes, and the overall vibe to fit the look and feel you're going for.

» **Beautify** adjusts your image in the TikTok by allowing you to add virtual makeup our adjust parts of your face. While it's up to you whether or not you want to use beauty mode, remember you're already in beauty mode by existing.

» **Timer** starts a countdown to give you 3 to 10 seconds before the video starts recording. This can be helpful if you want to set up for a wider shot or capture content with you and the group.

» **Q&A** lets you create TikToks in response to comments. Comments under the "Suggested" banner at the top come from the TikTok community, while the "comments to reply to" banner beneath it let you make videos in response to comments on your previous TikToks.

» **Flash** allows you to film content in dark spaces by activating your phone's flashlight to act as an extra source of light.

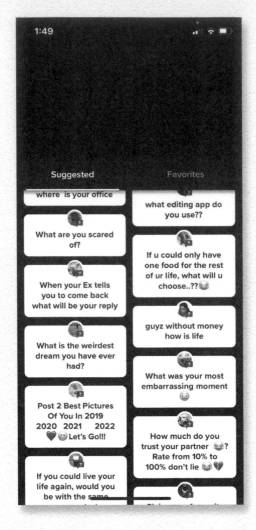

EDITING

Congratulations, you've officially recorded your TikTok! While editing your video may seem like a lot of work, a lot of the TikTok magic happens during the editing process.

UPLOADING YOUR CONTENT

Your editing experience will vary slightly based on whether you've recorded your TikTok in the app or uploaded it from your camera roll. If you've recorded your content in the TikTok app and are happy with it, hit the pink check button in the bottom-right corner.

If instead you'd like to upload photo(s) or video(s) from your camera roll, hit the "Upload" button in the bottom-right corner and then tap on the buttons in the upper-right corners of each piece of content to select it. When you have all the content you'd like to include, hit the pink "next" button in the bottom-right corner.

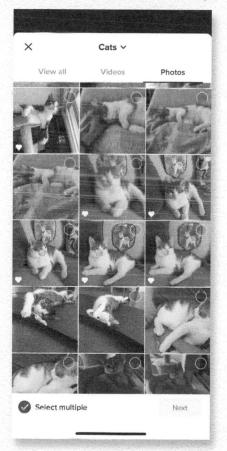

ADJUSTING CLIPS

To edit the length of your video, hit the "Adjust clips" icon on the right-hand side. Note that if you upload videos from your camera roll, you'll see this button immediately after uploading your videos. If you record your videos in the TikTok app, you'll see this option on the screen immediately after hitting the pink check mark.

SOUND SYNC VERSUS DEFAULT

If you upload photos or videos from your camera roll, the TikTok app will automatically "Sound sync" your videos, trimming them to align with your chosen sound. This can be a super easy way to edit your video. However, if you'd rather edit your video clips yourself, switch the toggle to "Default" and get to editing.

If you're manually editing your video, on the bottom of the screen you'll see each of your video clips side by side. You can:

- » Click and drag to reorder the clips.

- » Click on an individual clip to adjust the length — hold and pull in the edges of an individual clip to shorten it.

- » Pull in the edges of the overall video to shorten it.

TikTok will automatically play your video over and over while you edit it. Since this can be annoying (and mess up your editing), it's recommended to pause the video by tapping it once while you're editing. Once you've adjusted your clips, *then* watch it all the way through to make sure the video makes sense.

TEXT

Sometimes it's helpful to add text bubbles to your videos. These could spell out things like:

- » The names of different people talking in a video

- » Ingredients in a recipe you're making

- » A funny joke or story

To add text, hit the "Aa" button on the upper-right side. From there you can play around with the different fonts, highlight options, and colors to get the look that you want.

TEXT-TO-SPEECH

If you don't want to be the one talking in your video, but you want your audience to hear someone read your caption aloud, use the text-to-speech feature. To use this:

1 Type out what you want your text to say as described above.

2 Hit the icon to the left of the font options of the face with noise coming out of the mouth (shown in the previous figure).

3 From there you can play around with all the voices you can use.

Want someone to sing your text? There's a voice for that. Want someone to read your text in a funny voice? There's an option for that. Want someone to narrate your text in a deep radio voice? There's a voice to text for that too!

4 If you want to apply the same voice to all text bubbles you have in your TikTok, hit the radio button below that says "Apply voice to all text in this video." If you'd rather use different voices for different text, choose them as needed.

5 Hit "Done" in the upper-right corner and enjoy listening to whatever text-to-speech option you picked!

SETTING A TEXT TIMER

While your text bubbles may be helpful in one section of your TikTok, you might not want to have them on screen for the entire video. Fortunately, you can set a timer for how long each text bubble will appear onscreen. To do this:

1 Type out your text bubble using the instructions above.

2 After you hit "Done," click on the text as it appears on your TikTok.

3 You'll see a menu pop up; select the "Set duration" option.

4 Similar to how you edited your video clips, drag the edges of the pink box below to determine how long your text will appear on screen.

5 Hit the white check mark in the bottom-right corner.

TRANSITIONS

One of the most popular formats on TikTok is transition videos. See someone in pajamas? They snap their fingers and boom — they're dressed for the day. See a bowl of ingredients? The camera zooms in, zooms out and whoa — it's a full meal. Transitions are great for reveals and add a little bit of TikTok magic to your videos.

There are two major ways to add transitions to your TikToks. You can either use one of the transition effects on the editing screen or record them yourself. Let's go through both options now:

ADDING TRANSITIONS USING THE EFFECTS LIBRARY

Using the effects library is the easiest way to add a transition to your content. To do this:

1 **Upload your content to TikTok.**

   You'll see the best transition results by selecting content with a clear before and after (think: your dog as a puppy versus your dog now, before and after a big haircut, etc.)

2 **Go to the TikTok editing screen.**

3 **Tap the Effects icon on the right-hand side. You'll see a menu on the bottom of the screen. Scroll over to the "Transition."**

4 **Use the vertical white bar to select where in your TikTok you'd like the transition to appear.**

5 Above the menu, tap the type of transition effect you'd want to use. Don't like it? Hit the "undo" arrow on the right-hand side above the transition effects to remove the transition effect and add in a new one.

6 Hit "Save" to keep the effect.

ADDING CUSTOM TRANSITIONS

Sometimes the TikTok effect transitions just don't cut it. Maybe you want to use a custom transition, something like:

» Clapping your hands, which suddenly changes your outfit.

» Holding your hand up to the camera, pulling it back and suddenly being in a different location.

» Snapping your fingers in front of an empty room for it to suddenly fill with furniture.

To build one of these transitions into your video, do the following:

1 Record yourself in the "before" state, meaning before the transition.

For this example, let's say you're in your pajamas (the before) and clapping your hands (the transition).

2 Record yourself in the "after" state, meaning after the transition.

Now you're now dressed for a party (the after) and clapping your hands.

3 Edit your two videos so that the transition between the two is seamless.

This step can take some precision so be patient! It'll all be worth it when you have a TikTok with the smoothest transitions.

For this example, the clapping at the end of the "before" video should blend right into the clapping in the "after" video.

STICKERS

You can also pump up your TikTok by adding in stickers. Some of these are fun, like adding a pizza sticker to your video, while others can be more interactive, like stickers that link to a poll or to a fundraising page for your favorite charity.

To add stickers:

1 Hit the Stickers icon on the right-hand side of the editing screen.

2 Browse through all the different sticker options to find some that appeal to you.

Feel free to play around with them to find one or more options that add something special to your video.

3 Click on the sticker again to pin it. (This will keep the sticker attached to the item it's pinned to in the video.) Or set a duration for how long it'll stay in your video (for a refresher on how to do that, head back to the "Text" section earlier in this project.)

4 If you realize you want to remove all or some stickers from your video, simply hold your finger on them and drag them up to the trash can.

VOICEOVERS

Sometimes you might want to talk in a video, but it won't make sense to record yourself talking while you're recording the visuals. For example, maybe you're sharing a recipe video and you'd rather not cook and talk at the same time. Or perhaps you want to make a "day in my life" video, and are stitching together a bunch of different moments in your day, so you'd rather record your audio afterwards.

To add in this audio after the fact, all you'll need is TikTok's voiceover tool.

To record a voiceover:

1 Tap the "Audio editing" icon that looks like a microphone.

2 Tap or long press the pink circle button on the left-hand side to record your audio.

You can also tap one of the voice effects on the right if you'd like to play around with audio effects that give you a deep voice or make you sound like you're talking into a microphone.

3 Optional: You'll also see a button below that asks if you replace the original sound in your video with your recorded voiceover.

For example, if your TikTok is a recipe video, do you want to include the sounds of you cooking along with your audio (by keeping the circle unchecked); or would you rather mute the audio of you cooking and just include the sound of your voiceover (by checking the box)?

4 Hit "Save."

Great job, you've just mastered the fundamentals of editing a TikTok! Once you're happy with your editing, hit the "Next" button in the bottom-right corner.

TIP

Keep it short and sweet: TikTok audiences tend to have very short attention spans so keeping your videos as short as possible is a major key to success. We recommend keeping your video at least under 30 seconds, with under 15 seconds being the ideal. If you're stitching together a montage of different clips, try to keep each clip as short as possible (under 2 seconds is ideal).

TIP

Try to align with the sound: One way to make your next TikTok really sing is to match key features in the audio you're using with what the viewer is seeing on screen. For example, if there's a beat drop in the song, you'd want to put your more blah "before" clips as the beat builds and the exciting "after" photos after the beat drops.

MORE EDITING TOOLS

For most videos you make, you should have no trouble editing them within the TikTok app. However, sometimes you might want to take your editing to the next level. Here are some popular editing tools you could use if you'd like to edit your video outside of TikTok. This section will focus on editing tools that are completely free to use, but know that there are other editing tools available for an additional cost. Most of these apps can be found on iTunes and Google play.

» **CapCut:** This is an editing app made by the company who made TikTok. It's free and provides advanced filters and effects, trending stickers, and custom TikTok fonts.

» **BeeCut:** This tool is most helpful for beginner editors that provides additional filters and is particularly helpful with editing multiple video clips.

» **Zoomerang:** As another app for beginner editors, Zoomerang offers step-by-step tutorials for how to edit your TikTok videos. The platform lets you watch popular TikToks and then shows you how to make them.

» **Magisto:** Magisto takes all the legwork out of making TikToks. First, you can choose an editing style you'd like to use and then add in the videos and photos you'd want to appear in them. After that, Magisto will make your TikTok.

» **Funimate:** This editing tool is known for its epic range of video effects. (They have more than 100 effects, *and* you can use the app to make your own effects.) Keep in mind, though, that the free version would put the Funimate watermark (a graphic on the screen with the TikTok logo) on your TikTok videos.

» **InShot:** Since TikTok's in app editor doesn't let you import your own music, many users turn to external tools to import their own. InShot lets you import your own music or choose music from their library. They also have other cool editing tools like background blurs and new effects and filters. Like with Funimate, however, all videos edited in the free version of the app are watermarked.

» **Lomotif:** With this app, you can find and use unique, up-and-coming music in your TikTok videos. The tool has a massive music library that contains everything from major hits and unique songs to additional filters and editing effects. However, free videos are watermarked and users are not able to choose which part of a song is synced with their video.

UPLOADING YOUR TIKTOK

You've made your plan, you recorded some unique content, you edited your heart out, and now you're almost done! Here are the last few things you need to know before hitting "Post."

VIDEO DESCRIPTION

A good video description is the cherry on top of your TikTok sundae. While not necessary, they're definitely recommended for engaging your audience and adding an extra pop to your video. While you might have a description off the top of your head, here are some quick tips for writing the perfect one:

» **Lean into trending TikTok language:** Look at current captions on your feed and see whether they use trending words or phrases you can use in yours (think: "CEO of . . .," "becoming 'that girl' of . . .," or "POV (point of view). . ."

» **Ask for comments:** A great way to increase engagement with your TikTok is to use a video description to ask viewers to comment something below. If you're telling a story, ask whether something similar has happened to them. If you're sharing content from vacation, ask where you should go next. If you're sharing a cute video of your cat, ask if they have any cute pets.

» **Wait for it:** To encourage viewers to watch your TikTok to the end, use your video description to "hint at" a big reveal or surprise. Only do this, of course, if your TikTok does have a big surprise or reveal at the end because baiting your audience to let them down won't win you many followers.

» **Use it for instructions:** If you're shooting a tutorial-style video, putting more detailed instructions in the video description can be helpful for your audience.

TIP

When in doubt, keep captions short! TikTok is mainly a visual platform so unless you have a specific reason for a longer caption, like including directions for a recipe, try to keep it to a short sentence.

HASHTAGS

Hashtags are important for helping your video do well in the algorithm and be easily searchable. It's generally recommended that you add at least three different hashtags to your caption. When brainstorming what hashtags to use, consider:

» **The genre of content you're making:** Typically, you'll want to use hashtags associated with the type of content you're posting about. For example, if you're sharing a TikTok of your new puppy, consider using #puppy, #dogsoftiktok, or #petsoftiktok.

» **What type of content you're making:** Often certain content styles will have their own hashtags with tons of views. Examples include: #prank, #GRWM (Get Ready with Me), #dayinthelife, and #storytime. Think about whether your video falls into one of the big content styles (for example, fashion, sports, cooking, animals, etc.) on TikTok and add the hashtag.

» **What groups you fall into:** TikTokers also use hashtags to share more about themselves. For instance, if you're sharing a video about your love for Justin Bieber, you might add #Belieber to your caption. Or if you're sharing a TikTok of a new recipe you tried, maybe you'd add #foodie.

When you're posting your video, you'll be offered a suggested list of hashtags to add. The hashtags with a blue thumbs-up next to them are current hashtag challenges (HTCs.)

TIP

Always use #fyp in your caption! This can help boost your TikTok on the For You page. Although it's never been proven, a lot of folks seem to think so!

REMEMBER

SETTING YOUR THUMBNAIL

An important but often overlooked part of uploading your TikTok is setting your thumbnail. This is the initial image that audiences see when they go to your profile and look at your TikToks. You want this to be as appealing as possible to encourage people to watch your TikTok.

To select your thumbnail, you'll want to:

1 **Hit the "select cover" in the upper-right corner of the Post screen.**

2 **Use the pink outlined box to select which frame in your TikTok you'd like to serve as your thumbnail.**

   Consider using the most exciting image. For example, if you're shooting transformational (before and after) content, get audiences excited by teasing the "after" images.

3 **Add text to your thumbnail, if you'd like.**

   This will give viewers a sense of what each video is about before they click on it, meaning they'll be more engaged with each video because they're already interested in your topic. You don't need to put in a lot of information, but a quick summary like "best lasagna ever" or "my dog's cutest moments" should do the trick.

4 **Hit "Save" once you're happy with the thumbnail and get ready to post your TikTok!**

PRIVACY SETTINGS

Before you post your video, scroll down to the section on the posting screen that asks "Who can watch this video" to make sure that only people you want to watch your TikTok can see it. You can allow just your TikTok friends to watch, allow everyone to watch, or if you'd just like to post it for yourself. You can also toggle whether audience members can stitch, comment, or duet your video. Since you're under the age of 18, talk to a parent or guardian about these privacy settings to make sure you're posting in the best way for you.

CLOSE CAPTIONS

If there's any audio in your video, you'll likely want to add captions to it. This type of caption is different than the sentence or two you just brainstormed above to add to your video. These types of captions act as subtitles, writing out everything the people are saying or singing in your TikTok so that people who aren't able to listen to it can still understand what's happening. Today, most TikToks automatically add captions when you post. If you want to make sure closed captions are on or off hit the "more options" button on the posting screen. There you can toggle automatic captions on or off and select what language you'd like for them to appear in.

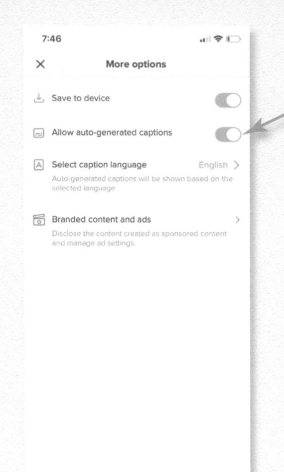

POSTING TO OTHER PLATFORMS

At the bottom of the posting screen, you'll see a section that says "Automatically share to" and icons of other social platforms. You'll see a green message bubble to share via text message, a rainbow camera icon for Instagram, a rainbow "+" icon to share to Instagram Stories, and a yellow ghost icon to share to Snapchat. You can select to post to as many other platforms as you'd like (or none at all). After posting your video, a pop-up screen will show you how to share your TikTok on other platforms.

Sharing your TikTok to other platforms can be a great way to drive views for your TikTok. This helps let your audience on Snapchat and Instagram know that you're posting to TikTok and encourages them to follow you to the platform.

Social media platforms are limited to people 13 and over. If you're under 13 you might not be able to post to other platforms if they have age restrictions for this type of feature.

REMEMBER

TOP CREATIVE TIPS

There aren't any official rules on how to make great TikToks, but there are some great creative principles, tips, and tricks to keep in mind so you can ensure you're making videos people will really love and that will perform well. Getting likes and followers isn't everything in life, but it's nice to know when your videos are seen.

BRING THE ENERGY

More than any other tip, bringing the energy to your TikToks is crucially important. It's a surefire way of engaging people, whereas being "flat" with your energy will likely have them scrolling past your video. You want to start your TikTok out with energy and keep it throughout. You don't need to be "one note," meaning that you stay hyped at the same intense level through the video; rather, you can modify your energy, adjusting it up and down as you go. If you want people to watch your TikTok, they need to believe you were hyped to make it.

TIP

It might feel silly at first, but a lot of people who appear on a stage or in front of a camera will hype themselves up first beforehand so they can ensure their energy is "up" when the camera is rolling. So, before you hit record, look at yourself in the mirror and tell yourself some affirmations such as "You've got this. You're a great person! You make great TikToks! People love your content." See if you can get yourself hyped up. Ready? Hit record!

ENCOURAGE REWATCHES

Lots of TikToks are watched more than once. That's a key feature of the platform — that TikToks are watched many times. The best TikToks are watched multiple times, and there are some smart ways to encourage those rewatches.

» **Add in background extras.** You can plan out your TikTok, then add in extras. For example, if you're dancing in the foreground of the video, maybe you have a friend dancing or doing something different that's interesting happening in the background. People will watch the TikTok looking at you in the foreground first, and then rewatch the TikTok watching the background action.

» **Wait till you see it.** A popular technique is to add a text overlay saying "Wait till the end" or "Wait till you see it," which can be an effective way to keep people watching. Just be aware that it could also turn people away. Some TikToks don't really have a "pay off" at the end, so people might not trust that there's going to be something good that's worth the wait. Use this technique only when there's something actually worth waiting for!

» **Ask for comments.** If you've made a video that is sure to encourage comments — for example, perhaps you're posting an opinion on a topic, like your unique perspective on the latest video game that's sure to spark debate, you'll likely get more rewatches as people want to see comments from other folks, keeping the video playing in the background.

» **The Content Flash.** Imagine a GRWM (Get Ready with Me) video where the final look is flashed at the start of the video very briefly, and very briefly at the end too. It seamlessly loops but because the final look, which is the pay off of the video, is flashed so quickly, it encourages people to rewatch the video again (and even pause on the final screen.)

REMEMBER

If in doubt, try making shorter videos. It's much easier to get a rewatch on a 30 second video than it is a 10-minute-long video.

TIP

Look for TikTokers participating in communities on other platforms like Reddit who share experimental and advanced tips and tricks for encouraging rewatches. New ideas are being created all the time.

EXPERIMENT OFTEN

Don't feel disheartened if your first attempts at making a TikTok aren't what you would consider especially good. It takes time to hone your skills and get really confident. Don't give up! Instead make lots of different kinds of TikToks to see what you like, what you don't like, and most importantly what your audience does and does not like. Project 3 has lots of popular types of TikToks to make. Try making a broader selection of them and see what happens.

GRAB THEIR ATTENTION

This is super important. You need to grab the viewer's attention in the first second or so. Just think about how you use TikTok. You're watching and scrolling, and if something doesn't seem to be interesting to you, you scroll past it really quickly. That's how much time you've got to capture someone's attention.

There are tons of different ways to grab people's attention, but here are some you can try:

» **Striking visuals.** Whatever your visuals are, making sure that they are striking can help snag attention. Striking could mean bold in color and contrast, it could mean a fast series of visuals with quick cuts, or it could be something unexpected — think of all those TikTokers who make videos of their magic. You might be surprised to learn that your face is the best way to grab someone's attention. You're more likely to grab someone's attention if your face is close to and facing the camera than if, say, your video starts with a scene of a field of cows.

» **Striking sounds.** Sound is one of the top ways to get attention. If you're using an existing sound, think of what will match your video best. It can be tempting just to use any trending sound, but it's better if it matches to your content. You can, of course, make your own original sounds.

» **Text overlay.** Text is a big part of TikTok too. Try adding text to your videos as this will help grab and hold a viewer's attention.

TIP

TikTok is a sight, sound, and motion platform, so make use of all of these elements to maximize your video's potential.

MAKE IT BINGEABLE

A very popular creative choice is to make your videos into a series that someone can binge. The idea here is simple. Make a video and tell people in the video that there is another part. Post the next part in the comments and pin that comment. Repeat this as many times as you need based on however many parts you have. You can make a video with as many parts as you like.

However, you don't have to make a video with lots of parts, especially as TikTok allows videos to be up to 10 minutes long. Instead, another way to make content bingeable is to make an ongoing series of videos. For example, let's say you're making GWRM videos. You could make one of these every day showing your outfit of the day. You can then add these to a playlist so someone could watch all your GWRM videos in one place. To add videos to a playlist, follow these steps:

1 **In your TikTok app, go to your video that you want to use to create a playlist.**

   Keep in mind, you can only create a playlist with your public videos.

2 **Tap the three-dot icon on the right of the video or press and hold down the video.**

3 **Follow the steps in the app to name your playlist and add videos.**

TIP

Making use of playlists is highly recommended to keep your content organized and easy for people to discover and enjoy. But note that at the time of writing, not everyone had this feature. If you don't have it yet, check back after each app update, as it's being rolled out across all accounts.

LISTEN TO COMMENTS

Listening to constructive comments is a great way to get feedback on the content you're making, so you can make it better. Remember not to take things too personally. Their engagement with your video is welcome because their comment probably helped your video be seen by more people, so thank them silently and move on. If someone is critical, try to look through any negativity to see if there's something helpful to you. If someone is being intentionally negative and unhelpful, just ignore that comment. Listen to comments that are helpful to you, but remember you don't need to listen or respond to every comment.

COLLABORATE

Is there anything better than collaborating with a friend on a fun project? You can work together to create amazing videos that friends will love. Working as a team typically leads to feelings of being more creatively inspired! If you're able to collaborate with friends or a relative who already has an audience on TikTok, you'll find that you'll grow your followers as fans of that TikToker might decide to follow you too. Whether you have famous friends or not, think about collaborating with a friend because it's the most fun.

To get started collaborating with a friend who also loves TikTok, consider the following Yes or No checklist:

» **"My friend loves to work together and is a real team player." Y/N**

When it comes to your friends, who loves to play on a team the most? You could collaborate with one or many friends — just remember that teamwork makes the dream work!

» **"We make complementary, slightly different types of TikToks:" Y/N.**

This is important because you want to reach people you might not normally reach. Look for friends who are TikTokers who make content like you, but who aren't exactly the same. If you make TikToks about dancing, you likely won't want to collaborate with someone who makes recipe TikToks — although it's not a completely crazy idea!

» **"I already have some great ideas on what we could make together:" Y/N**

If you can easily think of ideas for the videos you'd collaborate on, it's probably a good fit to work together. Think about what you'd like to make and see if you get excited about the potential collaboration. If not, it might not be the right fit for a collab after all.

If you've got mostly yes answers, then it's a good collaboration.

TIP

Ultimately, when looking for a collaborator, you're looking for someone who is like-minded and motivated to work together. If things don't work out at any point, it's okay; just say thank you and agree how to move forward from there. You don't need to force a collaboration if it's not working out for either of you.

Here's what to do next:

1 Reach out to your friend.

When you reach out, bring your positivity because you want your friend to get excited about collaborating with you. Let them know you want to collab, and suggest they check out your TikToks if they haven't already.

2 Get together to talk.

It's best to talk "live and in person" so you can get the creative juices really flowing, but you can collaborate over e-mail or text too. If you're feeling like you're on the same track, then there's a good chance this will be a great collab. If things aren't feeling right, then it's okay to not continue with it.

3 **Discuss different ideas together.**

This is one of the most exciting parts as you get to unleash your creativity. Check out the sidebar "Narrowing Down Your Ideas" for tips on how to be a good "ideas" partner.

4 **Focus on one idea.**

Once you've got a selection of ideas, start to pick and choose your favorites until you find one that you both would like to try. Start to think about the details of that specific idea; what items will you need to gather or plan for in order to make the TikTok. This is the time to figure out the creative details.

5 **Set a time to record the video.**

Set a time when you and your collaborator can make the TikTok. You don't have to necessarily make a TikTok where you're both physically together but that's usually best. Instead, you could each film your videos separately and bring your videos together in the editing phase.

6 **Record and edit your TikTok.**

Make sure you talk about who will be responsible for the editing of the TikTok. Ideally, you'll share the work involved in creating the video.

7 **Set a time and date to post your TikTok.**

When you post your TikTok, whoever is posting should make sure they promote the other person's TikTok profile wherever possible. For example, it could be a shout out to follow in the TikTok itself, in the caption for the video; or it could be a *link in bio* to your profile. At the time of writing, TikTok doesn't allow tagging another user directly in a video.

A link-in-bio is one of the ways you can link out from your TikTok to another destination. A very popular way to add a link to your bio is to use a link-in-bio service. It's a single link that clicks through to a list of more links, so you can send people to your other social profiles and any other things you might have like your creative projects or friend's pages.

TIP

One of you should post the TikTok to their channel, rather than both of you posting the same TikTok to each of your channels. The reason is that TikTok, like most other video platforms, doesn't like duplicates of videos to appear. If you both want to post a TikTok to your channel, consider making two different videos — one for each of you.

TIP

NARROWING DOWN YOUR IDEAS

One of the most difficult things about TikTok is coming up with creative ideas. You can turn what might seem like an overwhelming task into a super fun experience that can help you make your ideas into memorable TikToks.

Here's a simple guide on how to gather all of your ideas effectively, either solo or with a collaborator, and find the one that works best:

1 **Begin with a brain dump.** Grab some sticky notes and a felt marker pen, put on some music if that helps you focus, and do what's called a "brain dump." This means you write down any ideas that immediately come to mind — one idea per sticky note. Then post the sticky note on a wall. You might already have some things in mind, so write down and post those ideas first. Try to capture as many ideas as you can.

2 **Find inspiration.** Don't worry if you don't have lots of ideas bursting out of your brain as the next step is to spend some time scrolling TikTok to look for inspiration. If you come across a video that you think you would like to make, write it down on the sticky note and post in on the wall. You can also save any videos that you like to your favorites. Look elsewhere for inspiration   other platforms like YouTube or Instagram, or even find inspiration in your daily life. Talk to your friends or follow a fashion, sports, or entertainment blog — inspiration can come from anywhere. At this phase, you're looking to create as many ideas as you can. Add these new ideas to your collection of ideas.

3 **Sort your ideas.** Take the sticky notes off the wall. Now re-post them back on the wall, but this time create two groups. The first group are your favorite ideas, the second will be ideas you quite like, but perhaps you're less interested in. These might still be good ideas, so don't throw them away — save them for later. You might be able to

(continued)

(continued)

make them better such that you do want to make them after all.

4 Improve your ideas. Take your first group — your favorite ideas. Take each idea in turn and see if you can make it better. Great ideas don't always come out of your brain perfectly formed, so give some time and space to each of your ideas to see if you can improve them.

A handy trick can be borrowed from improv comedy, where comedians use a "Yes, and" approach. For example, you could make a video of you doing a dance. Say to yourself "Yes, and . . ." to see what else you could add to the idea. For example, "I could make a video of me dancing." Then say to yourself, "Yes, and *I could be in a funny costume doing a lip sync at the same time*." Keep going further and say "Yes, and *I could include my dog in the video also dancing*." If you're working with a collaborator, take turns "Yes and . . .-ing" the ideas. Let the ideas get as crazy as they can be — you can always dial the idea back later. The goal here is to let your brain really think about all the things you could do. Write these new ideas on the sticky notes and post them on the wall next to the original idea. You'll now have a group of your favorite ideas but with improvements added.

5 Pick your shared favorite. If you're working with a collaborator, now is the time to come to an agreement on which idea is the best one that you'd like to make.

TIP

Pets are Internet GOLD. Dogs and cats are especially great for TikTok videos because people love watching TikToks with animals. If you're using your pet in your TikToks, remember to prioritize their safety and don't take any risks. They won't be able to give you verbal permission to be in the TikTok, but try looking in your pet's eyes to see if you have a shared understanding that they are onboard with this. Don't be jealous if they become more famous than you; it happens easily and often.

PROJECT 5 GOING LIVE

AND 3, 2, 1 . . . we're LIVE! When your favorite TV or movie stars film, it's a lot like making a regular TikTok video. If they make a mistake, they get to try again. When you go LIVE, you're more like an actor on stage for a play, or a news reporter — everything happens in real time.

In this project, we tell you everything you need to know to take your TikTok skills to the LIVE stage.

QUALIFYING FOR TIKTOK LIVE

Before you start planning your big TikTok LIVE debut, there are a couple of things you should know before you try to unlock this feature on the app:

- » You need to be at least 16 years old *and* have 1,000 followers to go TikTok LIVE.

- » You need to be at least 18 years old to receive Gifts on TikTok LIVE.

You might not be 16 years old yet, and that's okay! As you become more familiar with TikTok and making videos, planning ahead for how you will go LIVE in the future can be a great way to get inspired and come up with ideas.

Also, why not have some fun and practice going live with a regular video? Try recording an entire TikTok video without any stops or edits — yes, even ignore your mistakes! Then, play back your video and see how you did. (It's just practice after all, so you don't have to post the video.) This will get you used to what it's like to go LIVE. Once you meet the LIVE requirements, you'll be ready to wow your audience with amazing real-time broadcasts.

TIP

Even if you are not yet 16 years old, you could practice going LIVE with a parent or guardian whose account meets the LIVE requirements. Teaming up for a LIVE is another way you can practice until you're old enough to do so on your own account!

WHY GO LIVE

Once you've mastered making regular TikTok videos, going LIVE is another opportunity to find new ways to express yourself creatively and connect with your followers. With TikTok LIVE

» There is no recording limit like regular videos, meaning the only limit to what you can do while LIVE is your imagination.

» Your followers get to interact directly with you, in real time, which can help them feel even more connected to you.

» Since everything is happening in real time — without any cuts or editing — you get to be *you*. Show off a skill, talk about things you like, or just hang out with your followers.

MAKING YOUR PLAN

Since engaging in real time means there are no re-dos, it will be important to plan ahead before you go LIVE. Being prepared means you will know what to say, what to do, and how to keep your audience engaged the whole time.

THINK OF YOUR GOAL

Before you go LIVE, think about *why* you want to go LIVE. Do you want to get to know your followers better, or let them get to know *you* better? Are you trying to get new followers? There are many reasons people choose to go LIVE, and thinking about what you want to accomplish is a great first step in coming up with a good plan.

Since going LIVE is different from sharing a typical TikTok video, think about how it's different, and how you can give your audience something new and exciting as part of your goal. Some examples could include:

» A special event that can only happen on a certain day. For example, maybe you want to celebrate your birthday with your followers.

» You want your followers to experience something at the same time as you, like unboxing a new purchase you're excited about.

» You just want to get to know your followers better. LIVE is all about real-time connection, and this could simply be your way of getting to know each other better.

CREATE A ROUGH OUTLINE

Don't think about TikTok LIVE like a performance; you don't need to memorize a script to make exciting live content. Instead, LIVE should feel more like you're hanging out with a group of your friends. This is about showing them the *real* you, after all.

That said, no one likes an awkward silence! Having a rough outline of your LIVE broadcast will make sure everything goes smoothly and you won't be stuck thinking about what to say or do next.

To keep things simple, try planning out your TikTok LIVE with a clear beginning, middle, and end. Think about how you want to start your LIVE and introduce yourself, then think about what is the main reason for you to go LIVE (or your goal). And finally, think about how to end the broadcast and say goodbye — maybe you'll want to tell your audience about the next time you plan to go LIVE!

DECIDE HOW LONG YOU WILL BE LIVE

Just because there is no limit to how long a TikTok LIVE can be, doesn't mean you will want to be on camera forever. Think about what your goal is, what your idea is, and how long it will take to get through everything. This is another reason why creating a plan/outline beforehand is really helpful.

TikTok recommends a LIVE duration of 30 minutes. However, you can remain LIVE for longer, or keep it a bit shorter, depending what you want to accomplish. Think about testing different lengths and see what your fans like best.

IT'S ALL ABOUT TIMING

People can watch your regular TikTok videos any time they want. They might visit your profile and watch a video that is days, weeks, months, or even years old! With LIVE, they only get one chance. Since you don't want to end up going LIVE with no one in your audience, it will be important to plan out the best time for going live.

TIP

One thing you should think about is, when is your audience free and more likely to be using TikTok? For example, you might choose to go LIVE after school when you know your friends and followers are at home and not busy.

GIVE YOUR FOLLOWERS A HEADS UP

People can be forgetful, so it's always a good idea to give them a reminder so they won't forget. When you have a plan to go LIVE, try posting a TikTok video in advance letting your followers know. You can also post on other platforms like Instagram. TikTok isn't a *chronological* platform, meaning you might see last week's content first, whereas Instagram Stories are real-time. Here's what you can include in your reminder video:

» The exact time you plan to go LIVE. Remember to include a Time Zone for your followers living around the world.

» Why you will be going LIVE (or your goal). This is a great way to get your audience excited about tuning in for special content they don't normally get to see from you.

INSPIRATION FOR GOING LIVE

Before you create your plan to go LIVE, you will need to come up with an idea that helps you achieve your goal. Think about how TikTok LIVE allows you to do something different than in a typical video. Your idea is what gives your audience a reason to tune in — and to stay tuned in when they join your LIVE.

Here are some popular TikTok LIVE formats:

» **Behind the Scenes (BTS):** Your audience has seen (and loved) your amazing TikToks, but they might want to know more about the *real* you. You can give them a tour of your recording space and show them how you set up your lighting, microphones, or background so they can see where and how their favorite videos are made. Or you could give them a BTS of how you train for your favorite sport, or how you prepare for a competition like a spelling bee or chess match.

» **Get Ready with Me (GRWM):** Some creators like to let their audience in on their day-to-day routines. While these videos are often focused on how creators apply their makeup, there are other things you can show your audience to tell them see how you do you! You can show them how you study for an important test at school, or how you practice your moves for your next soccer game. Whatever it is you like to do, let your audience see a step-by-step of how you get ready!

» **Ask Me Anything! (AMA):** Another way you can let your followers get to know the real you is by letting them ask you questions in real time. Maybe they want to know what your favorite food is, or if you have any pets. Letting people ask you questions and giving them answers right away can be a fun way for your TikTok LIVE to feel like you are just hanging out with friends, and your fans will appreciate feeling like they know you better.

Be careful not to show or tell your audience anything that should remain private. Make sure when you're giving your behind-the-scenes tour that no personal information, like your home address, is visible, as well as anything else you want to keep private! Also, remember not to answer questions with personal or private details about you (or your family members) during an AMA.

WARNING

» **A How-To Tutorial:** Do you have a special talent or skill? Maybe you are really good at drawing, or want to show off how to beat a tough level in a video game? Since LIVE broadcasts are longer than a typical video, you can take more time to show things off, and teach your followers a thing or two! Since you will be doing this LIVE, you can even help them by answering questions they have along the way, all in real time.

Not sure where to start with your TikTok LIVE? Why not try watching what others are doing? When you open TikTok, look for the "Live" button at the top-left of the For You page. Tap on that, and you can begin scrolling through other TikTok LIVEs. Seeing how other people create fun and interesting LIVE videos is always a good way to spark an idea for yourself.

TIP

SETTING THE SCENE

"Going live" means you can't make edits or re-shoot your content if it doesn't come out right, so it's important to think about how to make your LIVE broadcast look amazing before you start recording. Just like making typical TikTok videos, there are ways to ensure you are looking and sounding your best, which gives you and your audience the best possible LIVE experience.

TEST YOUR INTERNET CONNECTION

Having a fast and stable Internet connection is especially important for TikTok LIVE. If your connection is too slow, it can make your LIVE broadcast appear choppy — or worse. If you lose connection, your LIVE will be interrupted right in the middle! Making sure you have a fast and stable Internet connection will help avoid any issues during your stream.

TIP

Search for "Test my Internet speed" on Google. com, then click the button "Run Speed Test." It'll test your upload and download speeds and tell you how fast or slow they are.

FRAMING

The next thing you will want to think about is, what do you want to show your audience? There are two main options for you to consider:

» **Static Framing:** "Static" framing simply means the camera doesn't move. This is what you would use if you don't plan on moving your camera (phone) once you hit record. Think about your goal, and how what you want to show your audience fits in the frame. Be sure to crop out (remove) anything you don't want them to see.

» **Moving Frame:** If you don't want your TikTok LIVE to be still the entire time, then you will want to think about how you will move your camera around during your LIVE broadcast. Like other types of videos, it helps to have a shot list. Try creating a step-by-step plan of what you will show your audience — in what order — so you know exactly where you will be moving and when.

LIGHTING

Lighting is always important when you want your TikTok videos — or your LIVE — to look their best. Practice setting your phone up where you plan to record your LIVE, and use multiple lights to make sure you are well lit, without any harsh shadows. There are a few ways you can achieve great lighting:

» **Natural Light:** The sun is sometimes the only light you need. Try setting up your LIVE space near a window, or even try filming your LIVE outdoors during the day time.

» **Artificial Light:** You can purchase additional lights — like a ring light that lights up your whole face — to achieve great indoor lighting, even when it's dark. However, if you don't have these available to you. Try using the lights you already have! For example, you can use a regular ceiling light, with an additional lamp that's already in your home setup off-camera to help light up any shadows that might come from the main light.

» **Decorative Lights:** This is not necessary, but one way you can add interest to your LIVE space is by using fun, decorative lighting, like colorful LED light strips, fairy lights, or even a color-changing light bulb. This can add color and interest for your audience — just make sure that these lights don't interfere with your other lighting, as it's more important your audience sees what you want them to see.

TIP

Search on Google for "three-point lighting" and you'll find a professional but simple lighting setup. Three-point lighting is the best way to ensure you're well lit, as it uses two lights in front of you, and one light behind you. This creates a beautifully lit scene without major shadows.

SOUND

You want to make sure that your audience can hear you, or anything else you might want them to hear, as clearly as possible. You can purchase a microphone that is designed for videos, if you don't already have them for better sound; however, this is not necessary. Often people will use headphones with a built-in mic as a simple solution.

If you do not have a microphone you can use, try doing other things to keep the focus on the sounds you want your audience to hear. Do your best to get rid of any background noise. Turn off anything that might make a loud noise, like a clock or fan. And always think about filming in a location that doesn't have constant noise in the background that you can't control, like near a busy street.

KEEP PROPS NEARBY

You may or may not want to use props during your LIVE. Since you want to keep your audience interested as long as possible, you will definitely want to avoid having to walk out of frame to get something you want to show your audience. Have everything you might want to feature in your LIVE broadcast close by so it's easier to move from one topic to the next without interruption.

GETTING READY TO GO LIVE

When you have everything planned out and feel like you're ready, it's time to go LIVE! Just follow these easy steps and you'll be ready to broadcast in no time (Remember — you must be at least 16 years old and have 1,000 followers to go LIVE):

1 **Open the TikTok app.**

2 **Tap the "+" button at the bottom-middle of the screen.**

3 **From the Camera screen, "swipe right" on the bottom of the screen to switch to the LIVE screen.**

If you don't meet the age requirements, the LIVE screen will not appear as an option for you.

4 **Before you go LIVE, you must "Add a Title" for your stream.**

Your title has a 32-character limit, so think of something short that will be easy to understand.

5 **Optional: Add a new photo.**

When you are about to go LIVE, your profile picture will be selected as a default photo for your stream. However, you can add a new photo that is more specific to your upcoming LIVE stream by hitting the standard picture where you see the word "Change" — then, select a new picture that will give your audience a better idea of what they can expect to see in your LIVE stream.

6 **Optional: Add a topic.**

You can choose from a variety of general topics, like "DIY" or "Gaming." Of course, if you don't want to stick to just one topic, or don't know if your video will fit any of the topics listed, you can simply select "None" — it's all up to you!

This is a great way to give people an idea of what your video is about and can help you connect with audiences that have a shared interest with the topic of your video.

4:30

Doing my makeup for dinner! ✎

Change

\# Beauty & Fashion   ⚙ Add a LIVE goal

Add topic

Topics will help your LIVE videos reach more viewers and the viewers can use topics to find your LIVE videos, more easily.

 Beauty & Fashion

 Food

 Art

 Animals & Pets

 Pop Culture

 Music

Daily Life

7 Optional: Flip the Camera.

Just like making a regular TikTok video, you can flip from your rear-facing camera to your forward-facing camera on your device. You will want to make sure you are framing up what you want to show your audience before you go LIVE. All you have to do is tap on the "Flip" icon before your LIVE broadcast, and you will see your video switch to the opposite camera. If you want to change your mind once you're LIVE, or show your audience two different perspectives, you can do this the same way during your LIVE broadcast!

8 **Tap the "Go LIVE" button — you're now officially LIVE! Your followers will receive a notification when you go LIVE, and others can find your LIVE stream as they scroll through TikTok.**

Make sure you choose a title (and if you choose, select a photo) that are attention-grabbing. You want these to make people excited to watch your stream! For example, think of what makes your LIVE interesting or different, and use an image and title that can tell that story to your audience.

TIP

Consider using hashtags in your LIVE stream title. This will make it easier for others to find your LIVE!

TIP

USING ENHANCE, FILTERS, AND EFFECTS WHILE LIVE

Before and during your LIVE broadcast, you will have some options for what your audience will see, just like when recording a typical TikTok video.

» **Enhance:** One of the options available to you before or during your LIVE broadcast is the "Enhance" feature. Just as we covered before, this can allow you to touch up your appearance on camera including changing the shape/size of your eyes and face, or adding a smoothing effect to your skin.

» To use this feature for your LIVE video, tap on the "Enhance" icon on your screen, then tap on the "Enhance" tab and select any or all of the options you want to use. You can use the sliding bar to apply the different enhance filters as much or as little as you like.

» **Filters:** The option can help you touch up the look of your LIVE broadcast. Filters allow you to add colors, blurring, or other touch-ups to your video to change how it looks.

» To access the screen filters, tap on the Enhance icon, then select the "Filters" tab. Then, simply tap on your desired filter or explore different options until you find one you like.

» **Effects:** Using this option can be a fun way to liven up your LIVE broadcast. By applying fun camera effects and screen overlays, you can make your LIVE broadcast look great — or just have fun with the hundreds of cool, weird, and hilarious effect options you'll have at your fingertips!

> » To browse the effects, tap on the Enhance icon and select "Effects." Then tap on different effects to try them out — have fun experimenting until you find the one you want to use.

TIP

Be careful not to use too many filters and effects because you can make your broadcast look too "busy." While effects are a great way to have some fun with LIVE and give your audience something interesting to see as well, you might distract them from your amazing content — and you!

ENGAGING WITH YOUR FOLLOWERS

So, you've tapped the "Go LIVE" button and now you're streaming for the world to see. One of the best things about TikTok LIVE is you get to interact with all of the people watching your stream — so don't forget about them! Try to make them feel like they're part of the experience. They are there to hang out with *you* after all.

Some simple ways you can get your LIVE viewers involved include:

» **Say hi!** One of the easiest ways you can interact with your viewers is to make them feel welcome. Simply saying hello and mentioning their @ handle as they join your LIVE can make them feel noticed, and they will be more likely to stick around to watch your stream.

» **Respond to comments.** A lot can happen really quickly when you're LIVE, including getting comments from your viewers. Keep an eye on what your audience is saying, and try responding to them throughout your stream. It can be something small — maybe someone compliments you, and you just call out their username and say "thank you!" Just like chatting with a friend, interacting with people who join your LIVE can be a lot of fun — and make them want to stick around longer.

» **Try a Q&A (or AMA).** A questions and answers type of format — or "ask me anything!" — is a popular way to engage with your viewers when you're LIVE. This helps them get to know you better, while giving them the opportunity to be a part of your LIVE event. Let your viewers know they can ask you questions, then read the comments and give as many answers as you can!

TIP

When it comes to responding to comments, or answering questions from your viewers, don't worry about answering every single one! The LIVE comments stream can get very busy during your broadcast if you have a lot of viewers, and these comments might come in too fast for you to get to them all. Just pick out a few at a time and do your best!

» **Let your viewers take part in the action.** You went LIVE with a plan; there was something specific you wanted to show your audience. However, that doesn't mean your audience can't be a part of what they're seeing. Try to think of ways to ask your viewers to get involved. Maybe you want to teach people your amazing dance moves — ask your audience if there's a move they want you to do. Or maybe you want to livestream yourself playing a video game — ask your audience to help you change your character's appearance or decide what to build. Depending on the game you're playing. the options could be endless!

CO-HOSTING

LIVE videos don't have to be a one-person show. One great feature of going LIVE is the ability to co-host. This means that two different people can be a part of the same LIVE video. Just like a video call, both of your cameras will be visible on the same screen — only when you go LIVE, all viewers will be able to see and hear both of you.

There are two main ways to co-host during a LIVE stream: Inviting a co-host or requesting a co-host.

INVITING A CO-HOST

When you are the host, meaning you are the one who started the LIVE video, you will have the option to invite your viewers to co-host. This is a great way to get your audience involved with your LIVE, as you are letting them be part of the action. Other viewers will be able to see and hear both you and your co-host, so think about how to make your conversation with them fun and interesting.

To invite a co-host to your LIVE:

1 Follow the steps outlined in the Going LIVE section to start your LIVE video.

2 Tap on the icon in the bottom-left corner of your screen that looks like two circles linked together to see a list of people you can invite to co-host on your LIVE.

TikTok will show you a list of your friends that are also currently broadcasting LIVE. You can find them under the title "Friends." TikTok might also show you other individuals who are currently LIVE that have similar interests or a similar audience to yours. You can find these under the title "Suggested hosts." You can invite people from either of these lists to join your LIVE as a co-host.

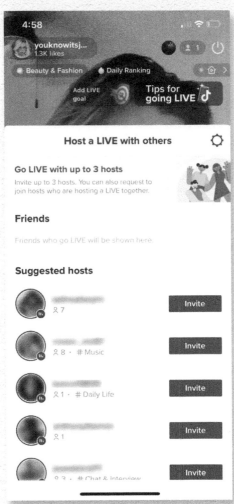

3 **When you find the person you want to co-host with you, look beside their username and tap on the Invite button.**

You will see a 20-second timer, giving that user time to respond to your invitation to co-host.

4 **If the person accepts your invitation, a small video screen will pop up. Whatever is on their camera will now be a part of your LIVE video!**

REQUESTING TO JOIN ANOTHER LIVE AS A GUEST

You can also join someone else's LIVE stream if you want. For example, if your friend is broadcasting and you want to join so you can interact with them on their LIVE, you can send them a request. It will be up to them to accept your request before you can become a guest on their LIVE.

If you would like to join another user's LIVE:

1 **Begin by watching the LIVE video you want to be a guest on.**

2 **While viewing the LIVE video, look for the icon at the bottom that looks like two circles linked together and tap it.**

You have sent a request to be a guest on the LIVE broadcast.

3 **Now simply wait for the host to accept your request.**

4 **If the host accepts, you will see your screen pop up beside theirs and will now be part of their LIVE broadcast where you can interact with them for everyone else to see.**

REMEMBER

To join someone else's LIVE video as a guest, you must still meet the requirements of starting your own LIVE stream. You must be at least 16 years old and have 1,000 followers!

GIFTING

Have you ever seen a street performer — perhaps someone dancing, or dressed up like a superhero, or playing the guitar? If so, you might have noticed they have something in front of them to collect tips from people walking by — like a basket, an open guitar case, or a jar. This is a way for people who see or hear the performer to say "thank you" with a small tip. That's just like Gifting on TikTok LIVE! People who create fun LIVE videos are doing something that is unique to them in order to entertain other people who are scrolling TikTok. Gifts are tokens of appreciation; they let people give a "tip" to people they find entertaining on TikTok LIVE.

While you might be too young for this feature right now, it is helpful to think ahead! Gifts are a great way to consider using TikTok as a way to make money once you're old enough.

REMEMBER

In order to send or receive gifts, or to purchase coins, you must be at least 18 years old. You should ask your parent or guardian's permission before buying anything.

COINS

TikTok Coins are what you use to buy Virtual Gifts on the TikTok app. When you are 18 years old, you can use real money to purchase Coins that can only be used on TikTok. These Coins can be spent on gifts to send to other TikTok users who go live. To purchase Coins:

1 **Open the TikTok app.**

2 **Tap on the Profile icon at the bottom-right of your screen.**

3 Tap on the icon at the top-right of the Profile page that look like three horizontal lines.

4 Tap on "Settings and privacy," beside the icon that looks like a gear.

5 Tap on **"Balance."**

3:23

Settings and privacy

ACCOUNT

○ Manage account   ›

🔒 Privacy   ›

d login   ›

Balance   ›

    ›

CONTENT & ACTIVITY

🔔 Push notifications   ›

📅 LIVE Events   ›

Ⓐ Language   ›

🌙 Dark mode   ›

🕘 Watch history   ›

🎥 Content preferences   ›

📣 Ads   ›

The balance page will show you how many coins you currently have in your account.

6 **Tap on the "Recharge" button next to your balance to purchase more coins.**

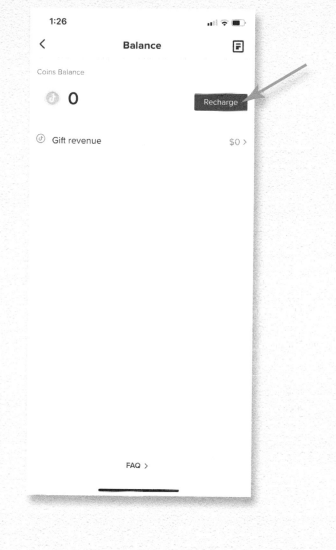

7 Select how many coins you would like to buy from the list that appears below, and then tap on the button to the right to show how much the coins will cost in real money.

8 Confirm your purchase with your preferred payment method, such as a credit card or PayPal account.

TIP

This section is also where you can exchange Gifts you have received from others for more coins. Gifts you receive are counted as "diamonds." You can also choose to transfer your diamonds to real money.

SENDING GIFTS

Any TikTok user (who is 18 or older) can exchange their Coins for Virtual Gifts to send during TikTok LIVE streams. Gifts come in the form of fun, colorful emojis, like a rose, a heart, or even a cute panda! Each gift requires a certain number of coins. The more coins you spend on a Gift, the more valuable it is to the person you're giving it to. Remember, Gifts are always a nice way to thank someone who is LIVE for being entertaining.

To send a Gift:

1 Start watching someone else's TikTok LIVE video.

2 At the bottom-right of the screen, tap on the Gift icon.

3 Find the Gift you would like to give: You can "swipe up" to scroll through a variety of Gifts. The cost (number of coins) will be shown underneath the Gift icon.

4 **Assuming you have enough Coins, tap on the Gift.**

If you tap on a Gift but don't have enough Coins, you might see a prompt to purchase more Coins. Ask a parent or guardian first. You can also tap on the "Recharge" button at the bottom-right of the screen in the Gifts section to purchase more Coins.

TIP

5 **Write a comment and tap Send to give your Gift!**

RECEIVING GIFTS

When you go LIVE, you can also receive gifts from your audience, who might want to show you their appreciation for your great LIVE content.

To receive Gifts:

1 **Follow Steps 1–4 (and the optional steps, if needed) in the "Getting Ready to Go LIVE" Section.**

2 **Before you go LIVE, tap on the Settings icon.**

3 **Turn on the "LIVE gifts" option!**

Once LIVE gifts are activated, your viewers can send you Gifts using the same method we just described in the previous section after you go LIVE. If you are the host, just focus on having fun and following your plan. Hopefully your audience likes your video enough to send you a Gift!

After you finish your LIVE broadcast, all of the Gifts you received will show up in your account as Diamonds. These can then be exchanged for real money.

FOR YOUR SAFETY

Even if you can't be a host of your own LIVE just yet, it is always important to put your safety first. Going LIVE can be unpredictable, since everything happens in real time. A LIVE video is like a direct link to you, so it helps to be prepared in case anything goes wrong or makes you feel uncomfortable. Here are a few tips on how you can avoid problems when you go LIVE.

DON'T FEED THE TROLLS

So, you've probably heard the term "troll" before. You also probably know that we aren't talking about the weird-looking creatures who live under bridges (no offense to actual trolls). We are referring to Internet bullies. Unfortunately, there are people out there that like to go out of their way to make things difficult for other people. When you're LIVE, a "troll" might send mean comments, or send comments over and over to make it harder for you to see comments from your friends or other people you want to interact with.

Here are a couple of suggestions for dealing with pesky trolls:

> » **Ignore them!** When we say "don't feed the trolls," what we really mean is to avoid them altogether. People who choose to be trolls want attention, and by ignoring them, you won't be giving them what they want. Eventually, they will get bored, give up, and leave you alone. Responding to trolls in any way during your LIVE should be avoided.

» **Mute a specific commenter:** Being the host of a LIVE video gives you the chance to control who can comment while you're LIVE. Similar to inviting a co-host, you can look for a specific user and mute them:

1 **Start your LIVE video.**

2 **While broadcasting LIVE, tap on a user's profile picture beside their comment.**

A window for that user will pop up on your screen.

3 **At the top right of that window, tap "Manage"**

4 **Next,** select how long you would like the user to remain muted. **The options are 5 seconds, 30 seconds, 1 minute, 5 minutes; or you can mute them from the rest of your LIVE video by selecting "Current LIVE only.**

5 **Tap on "Mute."**

Select duration

5 seconds

30 seconds

1 minute

5 minutes ⦿

Current LIVE only

Mute

6 **Tap on your desired length of time to Mute a user.**

Once you mute a user, not only will they not be able to post new comments, but all of their previous comments will also be erased from your LIVE comments section.

Sometimes, a person might just need time to cool down, or get bored. However, if you feel a troll is trying to harass you repeatedly, we recommend Blocking them instead of Muting them. On Step 4 of "Mute a specific commentor," simply tap on the "Block" option instead, and that user will no longer be able to view or comment on your videos on TikTok.

REMEMBER

» **Mute all viewers:** Sometimes, there might be multiple trolls, or the comments on your video might be popping up too quickly for you to deal with them. Luckily, you can mute everyone watching your LIVE video if you need to:

1 **Before you Go LIVE, or while broadcasting LIVE, tap on the "Settings" icon on the right side of your screen.**

2 **Tap on "Mute."**

3 **Next, just like when to Mute a single user, you can decide how long you want to mute all of your viewers. The options include 5 seconds, 30 seconds, 1 minute, 5 minutes; or you can mute all of your viewers for the rest of your LIVE video by selecting "Current LIVE only."**

4 **Tap on your desired length of time to Mute all viewers.**

WORKING WITH MODERATORS

Sometimes, LIVE videos will leave you with *a lot* to do! You will be trying to execute your LIVE video plan, while interacting with your fans, and also trying to deal with trolls. Thankfully, you don't have to do it all alone! TikTok LIVE gives you the option to use a "Moderator" — a person of your choosing who has the ability to make edits in the comments section for you, so you can focus on other things. Making someone — like a friend — a moderator gives them the power to mute people and remove bad comments.

To choose a moderator:

1 **Before you go LIVE, or during your LIVE video, tap on the Settings icon on the right side of your screen.**

2 **Tap on "Moderators."**

3 **At the top-right of your screen, tap on the icon that looks like a person with a plus sign.**

   You will see a list of your TikTok friends pop up on your screen. Beside each person, you will see an "Add" button. Only your Friends can be added as a moderator, meaning you must follow them, and they must follow you.

4 **Tap the "Add" button beside the person you want to moderate your LIVE.**

TIP

If you don't see the friend you want to make a moderator right away, try looking for their name in the search bar.

Now your friend is the moderator and can help to manage your comments section, including muting those pesky trolls!

If you think you'll need extra help, no problem — TikTok allows you to add as many as 20 different moderators. Just follow the steps above and select multiple users to assign them as moderators for your LIVE broadcast.

LIVE GUIDELINES

In order to keep you and other users safe, TikTok has a long list of rules to follow when making a TikTok LIVE video — similar to posting a regular video. As a general rule, think about being careful and protecting yourself. Ask yourself "am I saying something, or showing something, that I wouldn't say to or show to a stranger on the street?"

You should also think about what you are showing in your LIVE that might upset someone else. Just like you would in a classroom, try to avoid saying or doing things that are inappropriate, or could hurt someone else.

If you're not sure you're following TikTok's safety guidelines or protecting yourself and others appropriately, please ask a parent or guardian for help and advice.

TIKTOK CAN BE MORE THAN AN ENTERTAINING WAY TO STAY IN TOUCH WITH FRIENDS AND FAMILY. Many use it as a platform to gain new followers with the goal of having their content viewed by as many people as possible. Everyone uses TikTok differently and it's up to you to decide the content you want to create, the audience you want to engage with, and the number of people you want to reach. In this project, you will explore the hacks and tools necessary to increase your TikTok audience. Whether your interest is in makeup tutorials, food reviews, lip sync videos, or anything else, there is an audience for your content on TikTok. Use this section to help you find and grow that audience, and who knows, maybe one day you will become a professional TikToker who can make a living as a creator!

USING THE METRICS IN CREATOR TOOLS

To begin, it's important to have a clear understanding of metrics, which are the numbers used to measure results on TikTok. Metrics can help you keep a close eye on the growth of your TikTok account. Think of these metrics as a numerical snapshot of your entire account. Sure, your followers might message and talk to you about your content and what they loved, but metrics allow you to accurately see how your content is performing.

To understand the performance of your TikTok videos, look no further than the TikTok app. You can view all necessary metrics conveniently within your TikTok account.

Here's how you find them:

1 Tap on the Profile icon at the bottom-right of your screen.

2 Click the hamburger menu in the upper-right corner. (It looks like three horizontal lines.)

3 Select "Creator tools."

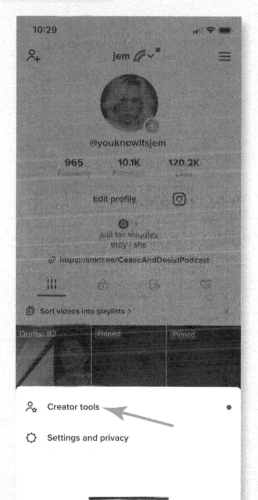

4 Select "Analytics."

From here you can explore your engagement metrics on the Overview page and more in-depth details on the Content, Followers, and LIVE pages.

OVERVIEW METRICS

The Engagement metrics on the Overview page are crucial in determining how much your followers are enjoying your content. Have you ever seen a TikTok account that has a ton of followers, but only gets a few likes and a handful of views? That's an example of an account with poor engagement. Sure, the account might have a large number of followers; but if people aren't liking or viewing the videos, it's a sign that the content isn't working. Likes and views are just two of the many metrics analyzed for creators to see how engaged their audiences are with their content.

The **Engagement metrics** include:

» **Video views:** The number of times viewers watched your videos.

» **Profile views:** The number of times your profile was viewed.

» **Likes:** The number of likes your videos received.

» **Comments:** The number of comments your videos received.

» **Shares:** The number of shares your videos received.

You can filter your analytics on the Overview page by selecting a specific date range in the drop-down menu. TikTok gives you a few **preset ranges** — last 7 days, last 28 days, or last 60 days — or you can add a custom date range. Just note that TikTok only provides data for the past 60 days.

10:30

Analytics

Overview   Content   Followers   LIVE

Oct 11 - Oct 17   Last 7 days ∨

Engagement ⓘ   ＞

▷ Video views
110 (+48.65%)

▤ Profile views
22 (+0%)

♡ Likes
3 (>999%)

☺ Comments
0 (+0%)

⇗ Shares
0 (+0%)

Followers ⓘ   ＞

10,109 in total
Net -7 in Oct 11 - Oct 17

Content ⓘ   ＞

1 posts

10:30

< **Analytics**

Overview Content Followers LIVE

Oct 11 - Oct 17   Last 7 days ∨

Engagement ⓘ   >

▷ Video views
  110 (+48.65%)

▣ Profile views
  22 (+0%)

♡ Likes
  3 (>999%)

Select date range   ✕

Last 7 days   ◉

Last 28 days

Last 60 days

Custom   >

Only applies to data under "Engagement" and "New followers".
Data displays in UTC time zone

GROWTH RATE

Growth rate is a more advanced concept that is used to understand your video's performance. As a young TikTok creator it isn't as important as other metrics that have been mentioned, but growth rate can be a helpful concept as you get more experienced. So what is growth rate? You'll see the growth rate in brackets next to the analytics in your Creator tools. Let's say you are looking at your video views from this week and it says you have 10 views this week with a growth rate (seen in brackets next to your number of views) of 50 percent. This means your video this week has 50 percent more views than your video last week. You can use growth rate to see how your metrics are performing now versus how they were performing in the past.

CONTENT METRICS

Content is comprised of the videos that you are posting on your feed. These metrics give you a snapshot of the content that you have posted.

» **Video posts:** Shows your videos from the last 7 days in order from newest to oldest.

» **Trending videos:** The top 9 videos with the fastest growth in view numbers over the past 7 days.

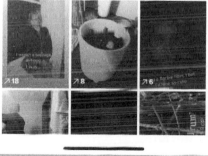

Want more video analytics? Open any of your videos from your Profile page, tap on the hamburger menu and select "Analytics" for detailed video data.

TIP

FOLLOWER METRICS

TikTok provides metrics about your followers. This data gives more detailed information about the follower growth (or decline) on your account and the demographic data of your followers. Demographic data tells you where your audience lives, their gender, and more information.

» **Total followers:** The total number of followers on your account.

» **New followers:** The number of new followers in your date range (selected from the Overview page).

» **Growth rate:** The number of followers you gained or dropped versus the previous date range.

» **Gender:** The male versus female split of your followers.

» **Top territories:** Where your followers live.

» **Follower activity:** The times of the day and days of the week that your followers are the most active on TikTok.

TIP

Beware of bots! You might notice that some TikTok accounts have millions of followers but low engagement and only a handful of videos on their feed. There are people who try to cheat their analytics by buying TikTok followers. For some, it may sound enticing to gain thousands of followers at the click of a button, but the great thing about TikTok is that it rewards original content and cracks down on bots. Buying followers is never a good idea.

LIVE METRICS

You can also view the analytics of any LIVE videos posted in the past 60 days (see Project 5, for more info on going LIVE). You will see this section on the LIVE page. Here you can see in-depth analytics on your LIVE videos, views, followers, and rewards.

» **LIVE videos:** The number of LIVE videos that you have hosted. You can filter them by the most recent LIVE videos, the most Diamonds, or the most viewed.

» **LIVE duration:** The amount of time you were LIVE.

» **LIVE frequency:** How often you went LIVE.

TikTok provides additional details about the viewers on your LIVE.

» **Total views:** The total views from your LIVE videos. This includes viewers who left and came back to the LIVE.

» **Unique viewers:** Number of viewers who entered your LIVE.

» **Average watch time:** The average time that viewers spent watching your LIVE before leaving.

» **Top viewer count:** The highest number of viewers that you had watching at the same time on your LIVE.

» **New followers:** The number of new followers this period versus the previous period.

» **Viewers who commented:** Number of viewers who commented on your LIVE.

» **Likes:** The number of likes you received.

» **Shares:** How many times your LIVE was shared.

As mentioned in Project 5, you can receive Diamonds as a gift on your LIVE videos.

» **Diamonds:** Total amount of Diamonds received. Gifters can send multiple Diamonds.

» **Gifters:** The number of LIVE viewers who sent at least one Diamond during the LIVE.

» **Viewer ranking:** You can see the top 20 gifters from your LIVE videos. You can organize by highest gift count or highest watch time.

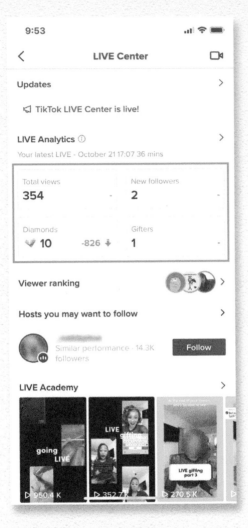

DEFINING A CONTENT JOURNAL

Making TikTok videos on a consistent basis is easier said than done. Sure, you could make videos when you have an idea and put it together on the spot, but it's easier and more helpful to organize your ideas into a content journal. Many successful creators use a content journal to help organize and plan their videos so they always have a variety of video ideas. A content journal also enables creators to align their content with current events, holidays, and seasonal trends. So, instead of doing one video at a time, a content journal gives you a thorough schedule for your videos; you always know what your next video will be. Preparation is key and will make your job as a creator much easier.

CONTENT BUCKETS

Before you set up your content journal, it's helpful to think about the types of videos that you might want to create. As you increase your TikTok presence, it's important to have a clear perspective and voice so that your followers know exactly what they are getting when they become a follower. *Content buckets* allow you to group the themes of your content cohesively. For example, if you are a beauty creator, you might group your content into the buckets of GRWM (get ready with me) videos, "try on hauls," "product reviews," and "tutorials." Of course, not all your videos need to fall within these buckets, but categorizing your content gives you some guidance as you create your content journal. If you get stuck and need an idea for a video, you can return to your content buckets to find a creative concept that is on brand for your account.

Some of the biggest names on TikTok use content buckets to group the content that they make. For example, Charli D' Amelio (@charlidamelio) is an expert in using the content buckets of "lip syncs" and "dance challenges" to create viral TikTok videos. Focusing mainly on two types of videos might seem constricting, but at the same time fans of Charli know exactly what they are getting when they follow her. Charli uses these buckets to add a unique spin to every video she makes. Another example is from Khabane Lame (@khaby.lame) who at the time of this writing has the most followers on TikTok — an astounding 151 million. Khaby uses the buckets of "shrug reaction videos" and "original characters" to create hilarious videos on the platform. He is specifically known for his iconic shrug reaction to videos in which other creators overcomplicate mundane tasks.

TIP

As an exercise, try going to your favorite creator's profile and determine what are their content buckets. This will show you that although they create a lot of content, they tend to follow the same themes. Make note of any videos that don't seem to match with their normal themes. Were these new videos successful? Or do they seem out of character for that creator?

MAKING YOUR CONTENT JOURNAL

As previously discussed, having a content journal is a secret weapon that creators use to organize and plan their videos in advance. Below are steps you can use to set up your journal. This way you can spend more time thinking of video ideas, and less time thinking about how to organize your own content journal from scratch. You will also see that we have given you a few pages of a content journal that you can start writing directly in this book. And when you run out of room in this book, feel free to follow the same structure in your own journal. Here's more info on how to use your content journal.

1 **We grouped the journal into seven sections.**

In your journal you will be adding the "Date" (days and times that you plan on posting your video), "Event" (any events or holidays that you might want to take note of), "Inspiration" (any videos you have seen that inspired the content for your video), "Trends" (trends that you want to participate in), "Content Idea" (the video idea itself), and "More Info" (any other information that might be helpful for you to add). The beauty of using a journal is that you can always add, cross out, or erase things if you want to change it at any point.

2 List the relevant events, inspiration, and trends.

In the Events column you can start adding in relevant events that make sense for you to focus your content around. A good place to start is by adding in national holidays, sporting events, movie releases, or anything else that is helpful for you to have on your radar.

For example, if you love posting about sports it would be helpful for you to know the dates of the Super Bowl or NBA Finals so you can plan content around these events. For the Inspiration column you can add videos that you have seen with elements that might inspire your ideas. This could be the way the video was shot, the content itself, or even just the way the creator acted. Lastly, it's helpful to keep an eye on trending videos, sounds, and challenges. A great way to grow your following is to create videos that are on trend.

3 Add your content ideas.

Now it's time to start throwing your ideas into your content journal! This part is more of an art than a science and where your personality and creativity shines. You can pair ideas with events that you listed in the Events, Inspiration, and Trends columns or just original ideas that you have that you want to add to your journal.

Content Journal

Date	Event	Inspiration
February 12, 2023	Super Bowl	Dude Perfect videos that show their friends competing with each other are always funny.

Trends	Content Idea	More Info
There are a lot of popular videos with football players being "mic'd up" during games.	"Mic up" my friends during our flag football game!	Set up one camera to catch the action and each player records their voices on their phone.

Content Journal

Date	Event	Inspiration

Trends	Content Idea	More Info

POSTING FREQUENCY

Full-time professional TikTok creators can post a few times a day. This might sound like a lot, and that's because it is. There is no right or wrong amount of time that you should be posting on TikTok. It all comes down to what you are comfortable with and what your goals are. If you are using TikTok to share fun moments with your friends, post whenever you feel like it. If you are looking to increase your followers, you will likely need to post on a regular basis to keep your followers engaged and obtain new followers. With more experience you might want to consider the number of times you are posting when you fill in your content journal. Many accounts that have gained large followings in a short amount of time are posting upwards of four times per day. Don't let that number discourage you, as it's more important to ensure that the videos are up to your quality standards. As you become more experienced with TikTok, you will find it easier to post more frequently while maintaining your excellent content standards.

TIP

Your TikTok can always wait. It's important to remember to not let posting TikTok videos get in the way of school, homework, or real-life interactions with friends and family. While your TikTok can wait in your draft, some of life's best moments cannot.

USING DRAFTS

One helpful tool on TikTok is the ability to save videos as drafts. This allows you to create multiple videos at once, and then save them for later when you want to post them. Let's say you love movies and want to create TikTok videos reacting to some of your favorite films from the past year. Instead of creating one video at a time, you can use drafts to your advantage by completing your video, but holding off on posting it until you are ready. With drafts, each movie review can be saved so that you can edit all the videos of your reviews once versus needing to edit each video right before you post it.

Here's how to save your videos as drafts.

1 **Record and edit your TikTok video by adding in any effects, filter, or text overlays.**

2 **Add your video description, tag other TikTok creators, or add any other hashtags that you like.**

   You will be able to edit this text, if needed, before you post the video.

3 **Select "Draft" in the bottom-left corner.**

   This will save your video to your drafts where you can choose to re-edit and post it later.

TIP

Professional creators always work ahead, ensuring they have a stash of videos on hand to post regularly. So, if they are unable to make content for some reason, like going on vacation, there won't be a gap in the content they're putting out.

UNDERSTANDING VIRAL VIDEOS

There are many reasons why TikTok is an exciting and innovative social media platform, but what really makes it stand out is that anyone can go viral. Anyone, whether you're a bona fide creator with millions of followers, or just an average person showing the behind-the-scenes of your life. This is what makes the platform so cool for up-and-coming creators, but also very tricky to master, because there is no tried-and-true success formula for going viral on TikTok. This section will focus on what it means to go viral, how the TikTok algorithm selects which videos to highlight, and what you can do to increase your chances of going viral on TikTok.

WHAT IS VIRAL

Videos go viral by being selected by the TikTok algorithm to be shared on the For You page. Viral means the video becomes really popular, with tons of views, likes, and shares. TikTok is assuming that the videos on the FYP will be appealing to you. As a creator, getting on as many For You pages as possible is crucial to going viral as it introduces your content to new eyeballs, many of which don't follow you. You may be wondering "How exactly does TikTok determine which videos get shared on the For You page?" To understand that, you need to understand the TikTok algorithm and how it selects videos to go viral.

TIP

The For You page is a unique page that everyone gets on their TikTok app. What makes the For You page especially unique is that the TikTok algorithm shows you the videos that it thinks you will like the most. Being on the FYP is a sign of a viral video because by being on someone's FYP, the TikTok algorithm is showing the video to people outside of the channel's followers. The more FYPs the video is on, the more viral the video is.

THE TIKTOK ALGORITHM

What do the Loch Ness Monster, the Great Pyramids, and the TikTok algorithm have in common? If you said they are each one of the great mysteries of humankind, then you would be correct! Well maybe that's a bit dramatic, but the TikTok algorithm is the secret sauce that makes the platform so unique and is something that TikTok keeps confidential.

An *algorithm* is the coded language that is written by computer engineers which informs how an application, website, or piece of technology functions. For example, Uber has an algorithm that determines the closest car to pick you up, and Netflix has one that recommends TV shows and movies for you to watch. Many apps on your phone use algorithms to make the apps function based on your individual needs.

Specifically, for TikTok, their algorithm determines how videos go viral and how they are shared to new audiences on the For You page. This list of rules is programmed by the app's developers to dictate how content is spread. There are pros and cons to this: One pro is that anyone can go viral at any time, and one con is that no one really knows exactly what the algorithm is looking for so there are no promises of consistently getting a creator's videos on the For You page.

USING THE ALGORITHM

Although TikTok keeps the details of its algorithm closely guarded, there is speculation about how it works. In spite of the fact that no one knows for sure, here are some items that the algorithm might look for in selecting videos for the For You page. Think of your favorite video game: You may know the ins and outs of playing it, but you might not know the behind-the-scenes details of how the game was developed by the game's designers. Similarly, the TikTok developers have created rules that are certainly important for the TikTok algorithm, but it's unclear to the average TikTok user as to what these rules are.

» **User interactions:** TikTok is always looking at how users are engaging with your videos. TikTok's algorithm is looking at engagement metrics to determine whether your video might be appealing to other users. To determine engagement, TikTok looks at metrics such as comments, shares, likes, rewatches, accounts followed, and videos created.

» **Subject matter:** The algorithm will scan your video information including video descriptions, sounds, hashtags, effects, and trending topics to match with the interests of users on the platform.

» **Technical information:** Elements such as video location, language, and type of mobile device will also determine the type of content that will be shared to specific users.

INCREASING YOUR CHANCES OF GOING VIRAL

Now that you know about the TikTok algorithm, it's time to see how you can use it to your benefit. Of course, there is no set rule book for going viral. If there was, everyone would do it. Trending audio is often used in viral videos during a set time period, but at the same time there are videos with no audio that have done very well. Not only does the TikTok algorithm change and evolve in its selection of videos, so does culture and how creators use the platform. What worked for some people one month might completely crash and fail the next month. So instead of chasing viral opportunities, it's best to focus on making content that you love, and then try to set your videos up for success by using the following suggestions.

» **Select trending audio:** Using trending music or sound can help your videos get discovered by a wider audience. See what's trending on your FYP and include that audio in your videos. You can also discover trending audio by going to the Discover page and then selecting "sounds." This will show you any sounds related to anything that you are searching for on the Discover page.

» **Insert hashtags:** Hashtags allow users to discover new content when they search the hashtag. In your videos, add relevant hashtags that will help your video get discovered by users who might be searching for similar content. Since there is a video description limit on TikTok, keeping it around three to five hashtags should suffice.

» **Add description:** Your description is another area where you can add personality and tell the story of your video. The TikTok algorithm will likely scan your description for relevant information, so phrasing your description to reflect the content of the video is helpful.

» **Have a strong opening:** Make the first 1 to 4 seconds of your content so engaging that users can't help but keep watching.

» **Make short videos:** Keep it short and sweet. Only use the time you need to make the best possible video.

» **Break longer videos into parts:** Instead of posting one long video, you can split your video into smaller chunks or parts to make a series. Instead of counting on one long video to attract viewers, you can increase the chances of one of the videos in your series going viral.

» **Use text overlays:** Starting videos with a text overlay entices users to spend time reading what your video is about and may encourage them to keep watching. Also, some users watch TikTok without audio, so having text overlays reaches more people.

» **Keep an eye on trends:** It's always helpful to stay up to date with trends on TikTok, especially trends that might be related to your content. For example, using the dance creator example again, it would make sense for a dance creator to make their own version of the "Renegade" or "My Money Don't Jiggle" dance.

» **Try to increase your posts:** Create and post as many videos as you can. This allows you to test your videos to see what content is appealing to audiences.

TIP

Successful creators test and learn by making different videos, seeing what performs and what doesn't, and adapting their plan accordingly. Don't be afraid to try and fail and try again — eventually you'll meet your goals.

TAKING A CLOSER LOOK AT YOUR MOST-VIEWED VIDEO

Imagine that your hard work has paid off and you now have a video that has more views than your other videos. What's next? How can you use that video to your benefit? And even more importantly, how do you replicate it?

First, it's important to determine what worked in your video. Sometimes it's a combination of a few things. First, check your metrics. Notice that this video likely has higher views, likes, comments, and shares than your other videos. Then take a look at the content itself. What did you do differently? This is why posting frequently is helpful as it allows you to compare your most-viewed videos with your videos that didn't work so well.

Review the comments to hear first-hand what people are saying about your video. Are they commenting about how funny you are, or is it your puppy in the background that's getting all the attention?

Watch any duets/stitches and see how others are remixing your content. This will give you a good indication of what is resonating and what components other creators find the most compelling about your video.

The next step is to try and replicate what was successful in your new videos, while keeping originality. For example, creator @thetreadmillguy went viral by showing three rolls of tape racing on a treadmill. Now, hundreds of videos later, you will see that all his videos show different cars and items racing on a treadmill. There is no question that @thetreadmillguy knows what content works for his page. This is a great example of how narrowing the scope of your content allows audiences to really know what to expect when they follow you. With that being said, you can still explore new ideas and videos to see if there are any additional content buckets that might help increase your followers.

GETTING PAID

Some creators can become professional TikTokers. A professional TikToker is someone who makes money on TikTok and may eventually consider it their full-time career path. Just as there are professional athletes who make a living playing sports, there are creators who make a living making content.

To get to this level, creators must grow a large community that is highly engaged in their content. For many TikTokers, the goal is simply to make and watch entertaining videos. Starting off with TikTok as a fun and creative expression is completely fine and making income on the platform might not be for everyone. If becoming a professional TikToker is something that you would like to do some day, below are a few ways that you could eventually make money.

Keep in mind that at 18 years of age you are considered an adult and eligible to receive TikTok payments. Teens who are ages 16 and 17 can receive payments with their guardian's approval.

Here's a list of how pro TikTokers can make money:

» **TikTok Creator Fund**: The Creator Fund is a program developed by TikTok to send high performing creators funds to help support their content creation. The amount of funds varies per creator and is calculated using a number of factors (mainly video views and engagement). To be eligible for the Creator Fund, TikTokers must be based in the U.S.,

U.K., France, Germany, Spain, or Italy; be at least 18 years old; have at least 10,000 followers; and have at least 100,000 video views in the last 30 days.

» **Partnerships with brands:** When you go through your For You page, you'll notice videos with #ad or "sponsored" written at the bottom of the post. These labels show that a brand has paid a creator to develop video content featuring their product or service. The biggest thing to remember as a creator is that you know your community better than anyone, so it's important to always stay true to your content and community, especially when working with brands. Additionally, you need to be careful about the agreement that you have with brands because they might want exclusivity, meaning you can't work with any of the brand's competitors. For example, if you're a makeup creator and a brand wants you to be exclusive to them, this means you can't work with other makeup brands during the duration of that partnership. Brands might also want access to your content for a certain period. Six months is the typical lifespan of a brand partnership.

» **Sell your own product:** You'll notice that many creators sell swag (t-shirts, hats, etc.) to their followers while others may even create an entire brand on their own. Emma Chamberlain (@emmachamberlain) is a great

(continued)

(continued)

example of a creator who developed a brand that pairs with her social media personality. In her videos, Emma often talks about coffee and creates her vlogs while going through the motions of her morning routine. With her love for coffee and chatting over breakfast, it was only natural for her to develop her own line of coffee. Now Emma uses her influence on social media to promote her Chamberlain Coffee brand.

USING AUDIENCE GROWTH TIPS

Now that you have all the skills necessary to monitor your metrics, organize and develop your content, and set yourself up for creating another video, it's time to put it all together to develop a TikTok account that can start bringing in followers.

In this section, you will learn the tips and tricks for growing your TikTok account to ensure long-term success.

COUNTING FOLLOWERS

As you think about the type of creator that you want to be, it's important to understand that you will face both opportunities and challenges as you start to gain followers. The reality is that social-media creators, for better or worse, are usually categorized based on the size of their following and not necessarily the quality of their content.

TIP

Although creators can be grouped and defined by their number of followers, it's important to remember that followers are just a number and that TikTok channels with large or small amounts of followers can still have videos that their fans love. It's completely okay to just make content that you are proud of, and as a general rule of thumb, it's always better to create the videos that you love instead of trying to make content for the sole purpose of gaining more followers.

Here are some common social media terms that are used to describe content creators based on the size of their following. (Note that "k" to refers to thousands of followers, and "M" refers to millions of followers.)

» **Micro (5k–100k followers):** Micro creators have something that larger accounts don't have; a very engaged and niche audience. Their ability to create unique content is the secret sauce that attracts followers to their account. It's at this stage where creators will also be able to apply for the TikTok Creator Fund (see the sidebar, "Getting Paid").

» **Macro (100k–1M followers):** At this level of followers, creators start receiving money from brands to develop content on their TikTok account. At this level, creators might expand their presence across other social media channels such as Instagram, YouTube, and Twitch.

» **Mega (1M–10M followers):** Having over 1 million TikTok followers is no easy feat, and it is rewarded with increased brand partnerships and increased money from the TikTok Creator Fund. At this level, creators might consider developing their own business or product to sell.

» **Celeb (10M+ followers):** At this level, a content creator is now absolutely crushing TikTok and on a rocket ship towards stardom! Brands are knocking at their door, not just for branded partnerships, but for more substantial partnership opportunities. At over 10M followers, a TikTok create could be hosting the Nickelodeon Kids' Choice Awards, joining a celebrity basketball game with Lebron James; the possibilities are endless!

PUTTING IT ALL TOGETHER

Now that you've seen what opportunities become available to you as you grow your TikTok audience, it's time to try some tips that are helpful no matter what size of following you currently have or want to have in the future.

» **Do what you love:** Yes, a lot of this project is about gaining followers and increasing engagement. None of these things matter if you aren't happy. So when it comes down to it, just make sure you are doing what you love. All the followers in the world won't make you love posting content that you hate. More important than anything else on this list, be proud of the content that you create.

» **Persistence is power:** Keep at it. The one thing that all great TikTok accounts have in common is that they regularly produce content. This is, of course, easier said than done as it's a tricky juggling act to keep posting content when you're going to school, doing homework and chores, and hanging out with friends and family. Just remember you can always decide to focus on your TikTok account later.

» **Always know your audience:** Use TikTok's engagement metrics to stay informed of your audience's demographics, locations, and interests.

» **Keep your bio simple and informative:** Most people will discover your content from seeing you on their For You page. When they tap through to your account for the first time, you should have a clear description in your profile bio of what they should expect from following your account.

» **Engage with other creators:** Collaborating with other TikTokers is a great way to get introduced to each other's audiences. You'll find followers of that TikToker will follow you, and vice versa. Another great way to engage with other creators is to duet or stitch their videos and to leave your videos open so other creators can duet or stitch your content. See Project 4 for more on collaborating with other creators.

» **Listen to content suggestions from your audience:** Keep a close eye on content ideas from your followers. If you see a top comment on your video saying "do one without sound" then your followers have spoken. You can pin the comment in your next video so that your followers can see that you are listening to their suggestions.

» **Stay on top of trends:** Try to keep track of trending sounds, hashtags, and content. TikTok is a very reactive platform, and you need to be ready to react to trends that align with your content.

» **Go LIVE:** Once you're 16 years old and have 10,000 followers, going LIVE allows for you to connect with your audience in real time. See Project 5 for more information.

GLOSSARY

Algorithm A social media platform's programmed set of rules used to filter, rank, and then direct content to users' feeds based on their individual interests.

AMA Short for "ask me anything," AMAs allow users to connect and engage with creators by submitting questions for them to answer.

Analytics The process of collecting and analyzing social media metrics, providing insights into your audience and the performance of your content.

Audience Current and potential accounts who follow you and/or interact with your content.

Audio effects A TikTok feature that allows users to alter their voices with audio filters including "Chipmunk," "Echo," "Megaphone," and more.

Bio The section under the profile image on each Profile where users/brands can include information about themselves and their content/products.

Block A feature that allows you to prevent certain users from being able to see your content, page, profile, and comments, or from interacting with you.

Bots A computer program designed to simulate a human, usually to inflate engagement, influence opinions, or spreading spam.

Brand A business/company's public identity and reputation.

Broadcasts The term used to describe an individual TikTok LIVE session.

BTS Short for "behind the scenes."

Challenge   A type of trend that encourages users to create their own videos performing a specific task.

Closed captions   Text displayed onscreen used to transcribe the audio portion of a video.

Co-hosting   A TikTok LIVE feature that lets users add another host or user into their live, with both users' video appearing split-screen style.

Coins   TikTok's in-app currency, used to send gifts to creators on TikTok LIVE and in comment sections.

Collab(oration)   When creators team up to produce content together.

Comment section   The section of each video where users can post responses to the content, engage in discussions, and interact with the creator.

Comment(s)   A type of engagement where a user(s) replies to your content.

Community Guidelines   The set of rules created by TikTok to establish a standard of behavior expected of users, in order to ensure a safe environment on the platform.

Community Guidelines Violation   Content or actions that violate TikTok's Community Guidelines, which will receive a strike. After three strikes, your account will have content automatically removed and may even be banned permanently.

Content   Photos, videos, or text — often posted to a social media platform.

Copyright   A type of intellectual property that legally protects original content.

Creator   The term used for a TikTok user who creates content on the app.

Demographics   Distinct characteristics of a population (such as age, gender, and income level), often used to identify which groups creators and brands want to target with their content or advertisements.

Diamonds   A virtual currency for TikTok creators that can be exchanged for real-world money — earned by receiving LIVE gifts from users.

Direct message   Communication sent or received by a user in a private channel, found in your inbox.

Download   A feature that allows users to download content directly onto their device, stamped with a watermark.

Drafts   Videos saved onto the device — privately in-app before publishing.

Duet   A TikTok feature that allows you to post videos side-by-side with another creator's content, which play simultaneously.

Effects   In-app video editing tools, used to alter colors, play games, and change your appearance.

Engagement   The measurement of likes, comments, and shares used to calculate the success of your content.

Enhance   The feature within TikTok's LIVE settings allowing users to smooth their skin, sharpen face shape, enlarge eyes, and apply filters that alter the aesthetic of your LIVE footage.

Favorite(s)   A feature allowing users to bookmark their favorite videos, sounds, and effects.

Filters   Premade templates for altering contrast, color balance, and other settings of a photo or video.

Follow   When you follow an account, you are electing to see more of their content in your feed.

Follower(s)   A user who has chosen to see more of another user's content in their feed.

Following page   A feed on TikTok comprised of only content from accounts you follow.

For You page (FYP)   A stream of TikTok videos tailored to each user's interests, including content from creators you follow and content from other accounts you may be interested in.

Friends   The phrase used to describe two accounts that follow each other. Only "friends" can direct message each other and see friends-only posts.

Friends page   A feed on TikTok comprised of only content from accounts you follow, which also follow you back.

Gifts   Virtual tips you can send to creators during a LIVE broadcast or in their comment section. On LIVE, these tips trigger an onscreen effect for the creator and other viewers to see. Creators must be at least 18 years old to receive Gifts.

Green screen effect   A TikTok effect that allows users to record themselves in front of an Image or video without the use of a physical green.

Growth rate   A metric that analyzes how quickly an account has gained followers over a period of time.

GRWM   Short for "get ready with me," a type of content that invites users to join a creator as they get ready for their day or a special event, often walking the audience through their routine, telling stories, and giving life updates.

Hashtag   A word or phrase following a hash symbol (#), used on TikTok to identify content on a specific topic.

Haul   A type of content where a creator showcases all of the products they recently purchased (usually a large number of items).

HTC   Short for "hashtag challenge," which is a brand-sponsored challenge tied to a hashtag. The goal is to start a trend and encourage users to create content using the hashtag and participating in the trend.

Inbox   The section on TikTok designated for notifications and direct messages.

Influencer(s)   Digital content creators with an engaged audience and the ability to influence users to purchase a product, or a take a specific action.

Lighting   The use of light to alter the quality, mood, and aesthetic of a photo or video.

Likes   A type of engagement on TikTok that shows approval of the content or message of a post.

Lip synching   Synchronizing (matching) mouth and facial movements to songs or other TikTok sounds, rather than actually speaking/singing the words yourself.

Live stream   A social media feature that invites users to share raw (unedited) footage in real time (live). See TikTok LIVE below.

Location services   The privacy permissions allowing TikTok to collect your approximate location to direct content relevant to users in your area. Users can turn these permissions off within privacy settings.

Loop   Editing a video so the ending shot and audio seamlessly transitions to the starting shot and audio when the video replays or "loops."

Mention(s) When another user tags your name in a comment, video, or caption, oftentimes directly using an "@" symbol followed by your handle.

Metrics Sets of data used to measure the success of your content in a variety of categories.

Moderator A trusted user who is given the ability to mute or block accounts and delete comments during LIVE broadcasts on behalf of the creator on livestream.

Musical.ly The social media platform that was acquired (purchased) by Byte Dance and became the TikTok we know and love today.

Mute A feature allowing users to choose to no longer see content or comments from other selected users, without having to unfollow or block them.

Parts (1, 2, 3, . . .) When a piece of content or a story is too long to explore in one video, users will break it up into multiple videos and labeling them into "parts."

Playlists A feature on TikTok that allows creators to organize their posted content into collections in order to make it easier for users to watch other videos in a series.

Privacy settings The section of TikTok's account settings that allows users to switch their accounts to a private or public account and change privacy preferences related to activity status visibility, suggested accounts and contact list access, location services, direct messages, and more.

Profile image The public photo that users will see associated with your profile page, content, comments, direct messages, and other notifications.

Profile page The page associated with your account, containing your handle, profile image, follower/following count, total number of likes across your posts, bio, links and the grid of all of your TikToks.

Repost(s)   A feature used to quickly and easily share any public TikTok to all of your followers. Your reposts will appear on your follower's FYP and the reposts of accounts you follow will appear on your FYP.

Retouch   The feature within TikTok's in-app camera, allowing users to apply a video filter that evens out skin tone and minimizes texture or blemishes.

Ring light   A circular lighting tool often used with a camera through the center to record videos with even lighting and reduced shadows.

Segments (related to filming a video)   The term for a single video clip within a full TikTok video. Segments can be rearranged with edits, filters, and effects applied to individual segments.

Share(s)   A type of engagement on TikTok that indicates a viewer has sent your content through direct messages, texts, a post on Twitter, and more.

Social links   Links that redirect to your various social media profiles, often linked directly through TikTok or in profile bios.

Sound library   A section within TikTok that allows users to discover trending sounds, explore playlists, locate their favorites, and search for specific sounds.

Sound sync   A TikTok feature that automatically syncs photos and videos from their camera roll with trendings sounds for an easy edit.

Sound(s)   The audio that plays alongside visual content. This can be an original sound, a sound from the library, or official songs by artists.

Sponsored   Content paid for by a brand or user to promote the post, either as a sponsored advertisement in your feed, or through a creator partnership — with sponsored content appearing on creator's pages, stories or LIVE broadcasts.

Stickers   A feature allowing users to pin digital graphics or emojis to their video.

Stitch   A tool that allows users to incorporate up to 5 seconds of someone else's content into their own TikTok as a way to respond or riff off of the other user's post.

Tag   Using a user's social handle in a caption or comment, which will then notify the user that you have mentioned them.

Tea   Slang originated from Black culture, meaning hot gossip, juicy information, or "the truth."

Text-to-speech   An accessibility feature that automatically reads lines of text from your video out loud.

Thumbnail   An animated photo composed of a few frames of your post, which can be seen on your profile grid.

TikTok Creator Fund   TikTok's program for compensating creators who meet the criteria for their content.

TikTok for Younger Users Experience   Allows users (especially under 13) to enjoy TikTok's features with additional content filters and limiting the information collected from them.

TikTok LIVE   A live-streamed section of TikTok, allowing creators to interact with viewers in real time and receive gifts from the audience. Creators must be at least 16 years old and have 1,000 followers to use this feature.

TikToker   A creator who regularly shares content on TikTok and has begun to build a following.

TikToks   A term used to describe pieces of content posted to the platform.

Timer A TikTok feature that allows users to record for a set period of time after the capture button is pressed.

Transition Seamlessly connecting two clips into one video.

Trend Content that has inspired many other users to participate and recreate or put their own spin on the original video.

Troll Someone who deliberately posts provocative or offensive comments/content with the intention of evoking an emotional response from others.

Unboxing A type of content where creators will document themselves opening a new package or product they've received. Unboxings tap into the excitement we all get when opening a new purchase, and they document the creator's first impressions.

Username The unique nickname chosen by the user, which is used to link to each account. Handles always follow an "@" symbol.

Video description A section on text appearing alongside a user's post, usually related to the content. This is also where the corresponding hashtags would be written.

Views A metric describing the number of times a particular piece of content has been viewed by users.

Viral Content, trends, or topics popular on the platform at the current time.

Vlog An abbreviation of "video blog," a type of content where creators document the highlights of their day or their experience on a trip or at an event, often speaking directly to the camera as if the viewer was with them.

Voiceovers Used to add context (explanations) or personalize your TikTok videos using audio recorded by the creator.

DEDICATION

This book is dedicated to Jacob Andrew Panturescu.

ABOUT THE AUTHORS

Who are we? Well, we're work colleagues who all, at some point, worked together at a company called Collab. inc, a leading creator technology company. At Collab, we developed hundreds of amazing TikTok video ideas for big clients, worked with thousands of creators and hundreds of big brands, and we regularly met with Team TikTok themselves to make sure we knew their platform inside and out. So, while this book isn't officially endorsed or affiliated with TikTok, you can feel confident you're getting quality advice.

AUTHORS' ACKNOWLEDGMENTS

Will Eagle would like to thank Claire Cohen, Andrew Panturescu, Hannah Budke, Andrew Cooper, Jordan Elijah Michael, Janelle Rae Salem, Daniela Mora, Eric Artell, Eric Jacks, Mike Crumbs, Sasha Panova, Donna Wright, Steve Hayes and the whole team at Wiley.

Hannah Budke would like to thank Grady Lawrence. Hannah adds "Can't wait to be your wife."

Claire Cohen would like to thank Pepper, Hobbes, and Finn, the best little TikTok rockstars there ever were.

Andrew Panturescu would like to acknowledge his amazing, supportive wife, Sasha Panova.

Andrew Cooper would like to thank his Mom and Dad for their endless love and support.

Jordan Elijah Michael would like to thank the Parcel Five and their parents for the endless love and support they've given.

PUBLISHER'S ACKNOWLEDGMENTS

Executive Editor: Steven Hayes

Project Editor: Donna Wright

Production Editor: Mohammed Zafar Ali

NOTES

NOTES